# DERRIDA

## OR BEGINNERS™

WRITTEN BY JIM POWELL

ILLUSTRATED BY VAN HOWELL

v

For Beginners LLC
155 Main Street, Suite 211
Danbury, CT 06810 USA
www.forbeginnersbooks.com

A For Beginners® Documentary Comic Book
Copyright © 1997

Cataloging-in-Publication information is available from the Library of Congress.

ISBN # 978-1-934389-11-9 Trade

Manufactured in the United States of America

For Beginners® and Beginners Documentary Comic Books® are published
by For Beginners LLC.

Reprint Edition

10 9 8 7

# DEDICATION

# For
# Michelle

# CONTENTS

# DERRIDA
## FOR BEGINNERS™

WRITTEN BY JIM POWELL

ILLUSTRATED BY VAN HOWELL

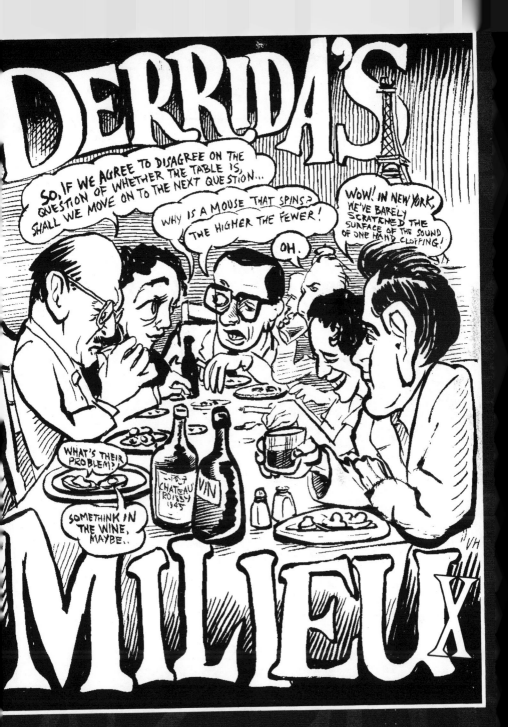

rance, for intellectuals, has long beckoned as a kind of paradise, a place where philosophers and thinkers have been looked upon as national treasures. For decades, on the sidewalks outside the cafes of Paris, light has danced down through the boughs along the boulevards, playing over the surfaces of objects, dappling tablecloths and variously attired torsos in swarms of ephemeral hues. Cafe-goers, many of them people of intelligence and culture, have placed orders, fumbled for cigarettes, and found it very attractive to be able to sit at a table and talk about the table and, raising a philosophical eyebrow in the dappled light, to ask if the table *is*. Such tabletalk has long overspilled the cafes and boulevards, crept in under the window sills and doorways of museums and galleries, studios and publishing houses, to permeate all the arts, including literature.

residing over all this tabletalk, from the time of the French Revolution, the image of the philosopher was one of the intellectual engagé, who, besides wondering if the table is or is not, was to be found immersed in political and public affairs, bucking the tide of established values, setting a moral tone, taking a stand, and—most important—being avant-garde. In recent times, up until the late 1960s, Jean Paul Sartre defined the image. But—then the icon of the intellectual changed.

At the same time young Americans were tripping to Jimi Hendrix, "Hey Jude," *Hair*, and *2001: A Space Odyssey*, a student movement swept across Europe.

French students, supported by the Marxists, took to the streets, fighting the army and police in order to overthrow the government. They nearly succeeded, but were eventually subdued. Besides, they wanted to go on summer vacation. Failing to demolish state power, they became disillusioned, inward-looking. Suddenly exhibiting a **postmodern** skepticism of grand myths such as Marxism and Communism, they began to commit themselves to language itself. Disengaging themselves from politics, they became **linguistic** revolutionaries, finding revolution in turns of speech, and began to view *literature*, *reading* and *writing* as subversive political acts *in themselves*.

**I**ntellectuals began attending to *how* words mean more than *what* they mean. Increasingly distrustful of language claiming to convey only a single authoritarian message—they began exploring how words can say many different meanings simultaneously.

But by the time all this had taken place in France, Jacques Derrida had emerged, in the late 1960s in America, as the most avant-garde of the avant-garde. At his lecture given at the Johns Hopkins University in 1966, "Structure, Sign and Play in the Discourse of the Human Sciences," he had caused a stir in American academia. His thought struck a new chord that caused many previous philosophers to be reassessed, and it set the tone for much thought to come. It was something of a disharmonious chord, for his forte was a subversive mode of reading authoritarian texts, or any texts. This style of reading came to be known as **deconstruction**. Then in France **deconstruction**, kicking existentialism aside, was suddenly much in vogue. Derrida became the philosopher of the day, the new *enfant terrible*, the new philosopher punk, of French intellectualism. And then, after the American debut at Johns Hopkins, deconstruction and Jacques Derrida took America by storm, turning much of the Western worldview topsy-turvy.

As we shall see, Derrida was not simply a French intellectual, for the milieux influencing his emotions, intellect, and career were neither simply French nor Jewish nor Algerian nor American.

# A Brief Biography

Whatever one's philosophical or critical orientation, no thinker today can ignore the work of Jacques Derrida. It was in 1966 that he was invited to present a paper at a Johns Hopkins University conference. What resulted, however, was something of a major philosophical coup. Derrida, quite unexpectedly, cast the entire history of philosophy in the West into doubt.

1966:
Deconstruction
Debuts

After this revolutionary debut, in 1967 Derrida burst upon the scene of writing with three books, *Writing and Difference*, *Of Grammatology*, and *Voice and Phenomenon*. Since then, the intellectual movement he spawned, known as **deconstruction,** has gained both admirers and detractors worldwide, bringing about a global change in the way many thinkers think. Derrida has published more than 20 books and numerous papers—dividing his time between lecturing assignments in Paris and the United States. Obviously, Jacques Derrida is nobody's fool.

But for many years, he was nobody's hero either. In 1930—the year the Second Surrealist Manifesto appeared; the works of Kafka, dead for several years, were emerging from obscurity; Hemingway was becoming widely read; Gide's *Travels in the Congo* was published; D. H. Lawrence died; "Singing in the Rain" filled the airwaves; and the photo flashbulb popped upon the scene—**Jacques Derrida**, son of Aimé and Georgette Derrida, was born into a Jewish family in El-Biar, Algiers, his childhood dwelling a villa edenic enough to be named "the garden." This domestic oasis, however, was framed by an environment where Jews were openly discriminated against— subjected to verbal and physical violence and prohibited from entering the legal or teaching professions.

At the Lycée de Ben Aknoun, which the young Jacques joined in 1941, he was expelled on the first day of classes because of a policy limiting Jews to only seven percent of the student population. In 1943, he enrolled in the Lycée Emile-Maupas, but dropped out because of the intolerable anti-Semitic atmosphere. It was, perhaps, the hostilities experienced during these years that awakened in the young Derrida a sensitivity to the more general problem of identification, of the *central* and the *marginal*, which would come to dominate his mature philosophical thought. From age 13 to 17, he returned to the Lycée de Ben Aknoun, temporarily housed in a complex of huts, as the main building had been converted to a prison-camp for Italians. Here Derrida became a sports enthusiast, dreaming of a career as a football star. Upon failing his baccalaureat, he became withdrawn, lost himself in reading Rousseau, Gide, Nietzsche, Valéry, and Camus, and managed to publish some fledgling lines of verse in small North African reviews. At the age of 19, he was a student in France, where (after a couple of failed attempts) he attended the École Normale Supériéure and married Marguerite Aucouturier in 1957. In the 60's he joined the fervor of intellectualism surrounding the avant-garde journal *Tel Quel*, an ultra-left publication celebrating, among other things, Maoism, surrealism, and the material qualities of language—its sounds, rhythms and ability to suggest many meanings. Shortly after that he was invited to participate in the groundbreaking colloquium at the Johns Hopkins University.

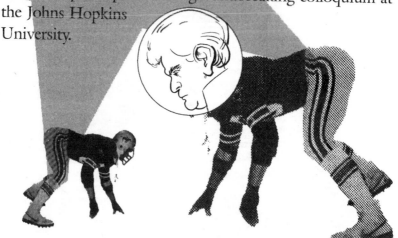

PARC de DECONSTRUCTIONISME

More recently, we find him, in 1981, engaged in a clandestine seminar in Prague, where he was arrested, imprisoned and then expelled from the country. During this period he also appeared in the film *Ghost Dance* (1982, directed by Ken MacMillan) and became active in initiatives to end Apartheid in South Africa. In 1986 he collaborated on a park project with American architect Peter Eisenman.

In 1984, J.D. and his sister visited their childhood home at 13, rue d'Aurelle-de-Paladines, in El-Biar. The Algerian owner was a very nice guy, but eventually it was time for the Derridas to go. The Empire and Eden ended except in memory.

If Derrida has managed to turn much of Western thought on its head, he has done so only by standing on the shoulders of Nietzsche, Freud, Heidegger, and Saussure.

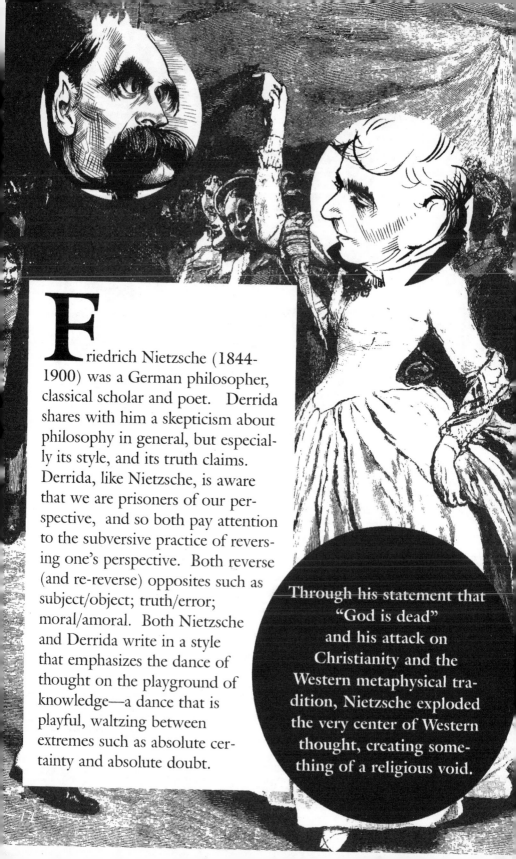

Friedrich Nietzsche (1844-1900) was a German philosopher, classical scholar and poet. Derrida shares with him a skepticism about philosophy in general, but especially its style, and its truth claims. Derrida, like Nietzsche, is aware that we are prisoners of our perspective, and so both pay attention to the subversive practice of reversing one's perspective. Both reverse (and re-reverse) opposites such as subject/object; truth/error; moral/amoral. Both Nietzsche and Derrida write in a style that emphasizes the dance of thought on the playground of knowledge—a dance that is playful, waltzing between extremes such as absolute certainty and absolute doubt.

Through his statement that "God is dead" and his attack on Christianity and the Western metaphysical tradition, Nietzsche exploded the very center of Western thought, creating something of a religious void.

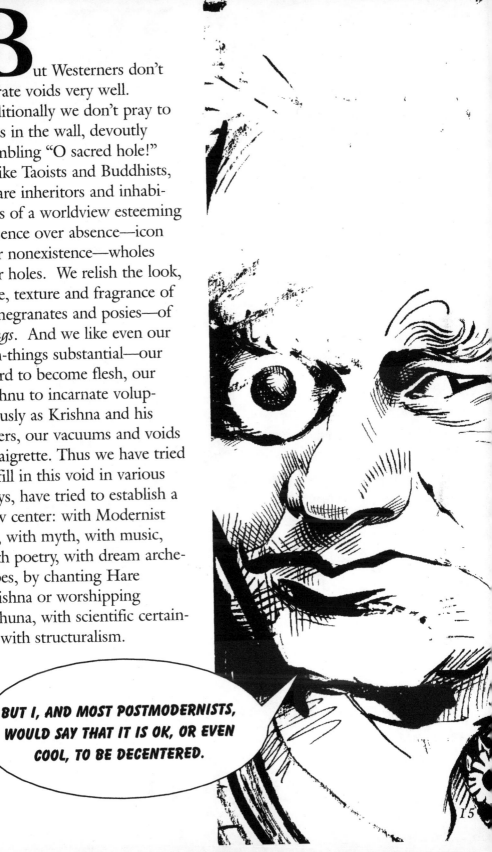

**B**ut Westerners don't tolerate voids very well. Traditionally we don't pray to holes in the wall, devoutly mumbling "O sacred hole!" Unlike Taoists and Buddhists, we are inheritors and inhabitants of a worldview esteeming presence over absence—icon over nonexistence—wholes over holes. We relish the look, taste, texture and fragrance of pomegranates and posies—of *things*. And we like even our non-things substantial—our Word to become flesh, our Vishnu to incarnate voluptuously as Krishna and his lovers, our vacuums and voids vinaigrette. Thus we have tried to fill in this void in various ways, have tried to establish a new center: with Modernist art, with myth, with music, with poetry, with dream archetypes, by chanting Hare Krishna or worshipping Kahuna, with scientific certainty, with structuralism.

BUT I, AND MOST POSTMODERNISTS, WOULD SAY THAT IT IS OK, OR EVEN COOL, TO BE DECENTERED.

15

**W**ith Sigmund Freud (1856-1939), the originator of psychoanalysis, Derrida questions the unity of the human psyche, which, always haunted by subconscious traces of past experience, always differs from itself—is always marked by difference.

**T**he word "deconstruction" comes from the German philosopher Martin Heidegger's (1889-1976) concept of *Destruktion*, his call for the loosening up of the old tradition of ontology—the study of ultimate Rock Bottom Reality—through an exposure of its internal development. Also, Derrida borrowed from Heidegger the practice of crossing out terms after he has written them. Just as Heidegger marked an "X" through Being (~~Being~~), Derrida followed suit with "is," allowing cafe-goers now to ask if the table ~~is~~.

**Why?** We'll get to that.

**F**erdinand de Saussure was the Swiss linguist whose structural linguistics formed the basis for **structuralism** in disciplines such as literature, semiotics, folklore, and anthropology. Saussure thought there is an abstract structure that determines all language's concrete manifestations, like the rules of chess that determine all the concrete moves one can make in the game. Similarly, structural anthropologists believe there are abstract structures at the basis of cultural forms such as myth, kinship, etc. This led to structural analyses of such various "texts" as: striptease, boxing, myths, political campaigns, religious rituals, and even traffic signals.

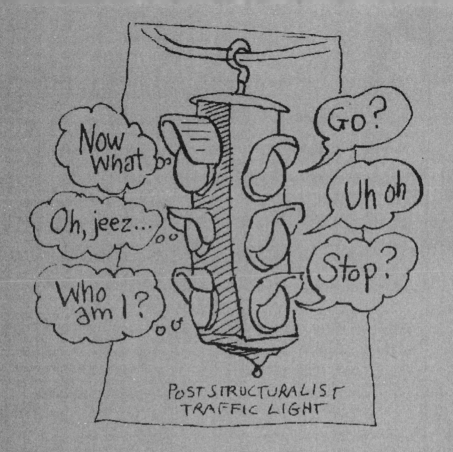

In such analyses the meaning of the parts is not so important as the relationship between the parts. For instance the meaning of the red, yellow, and green lights in a system of traffic lights is not based on the greenness of green or the yellowness of yellow. The meaning of the lights is based upon their relationship to each other as parts of a system. They could be replaced by any other colors and the system would still have the same meaning. A purple light could just as well mean

# STOP!

Structuralism promised to provide anthropology, literary criticism, and other fields with a scientific basis, but before it could ever make its mark in America, Derrida, the final speaker at the Johns Hopkins Seminar heralding the promise of structuralism, exposed its weaknesses. For structuralism depends upon structures, and structures depend upon centers—and Derrida called into question the very idea of a stable center. The era of **poststructuralism** had been ushered in.

Poststructure
(USA, CIRCA 1935)

**Poststructuralism** is a movement associated with a wave of French thinkers: Jacques Derrida, Julia Kristeva, Roland Barthes, Gilles Deleuze, Felix Guattari and Michel Foucault. Poststructuralists tend to see all knowledge—history, anthropology, literature, psychology, etc. as **textual**. This means that knowledge is not composed just of *concepts*, but of *words*.

AND WORDS, SUCH AS "PORT"—WHICH CAN MEAN EITHER "WINE" OR "HARBOR"—CAN SUGGEST DIFFERENT MEANINGS.

# What is Deconstruction?

*Why would one need to be DECENTERED?*

Well, defining deconstruction is an activity that goes against the whole thrust of Derrida's thought. Actually, Derrida has said that any statement such as "deconstruction is 'X'" automatically misses the point. But deconstruction often involves a way of reading that concerns itself with **decentering**—with unmasking the problematic nature of all **centers**.

*Oh, all sorts of reasons,*

*I guess*

Decentering? Centers? What is a center? What is problematic about one? Why would one need to be decentered?

Well, Derrida, when he is not deconstructing a text of some difficult philosopher such as Nietszche or Heidegger, writes about centers in such abstract language that I will offer you some concrete examples. According to Derrida, all Western thought is based on the idea of a center—an origin, a Truth, an Ideal Form, a Fixed Point, an Immovable Mover, an Essence, a God, a Presence, which is usually capitalized, and guarantees all meaning.

For instance for 2000 years much of Western culture has been centered on the idea of Christianity and Christ.

And it is the same in other cultures as well. They all have their own central symbols.

Well, what's the matter with that?

he problem with centers, for Derrida, is that
ey *attempt* to exclude. In doing so they
nore, repress or *marginalize* others (which
come the Other). In male-dominated soci-
ies, man is central (and woman is the mar-
nalized Other, repressed, ignored, pushed to
e margins).

If you have a culture which has Christ in the center of its
icons, then Christians will be central to that culture, and
Buddhists, Muslims, Jews—anybody different—will be in the
margins—marginalized—pushed to the
outside. (We must remember that Derrida was born into an
assimilated Jewish family in Algiers, growing up as a member
of a marginalized, dispossessed culture).

Want to PLAY?

Hell, no! Not until we get FIXED!!

FIXING THE PLAY
OF BINARY OPPOSITES
(DIGITAL MODE)
(dread of synthesis
forestalls reproduxion)

So the longing for a center spawns **binary opposites**, with one
term of the opposition central and the other marginal.
Furthermore, centers want to fix, or freeze the play of **binary
opposites**.

Freeze the play of **binary opposites**? What does that mean?

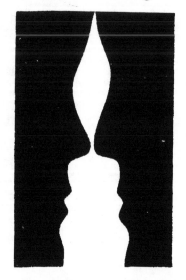

Well, the opposition man/woman is just one **binary opposite**. Others are spirit/matter; nature/culture; Caucasian/Black; Christian/pagan. According to Derrida we have no access to reality except through concepts, codes and categories, and the human mind functions by forming conceptual pairs such as these. You see how one member of the pair, (here the left), is privileged. The right-hand term then becomes marginalized. Icons with Christ or Buddha or whatever in the center try to tell us that what is in the center is the only reality. All other views are repressed. Drawing such an icon is an attempt to freeze the play of opposites between, for example, Christian/Jew or Christian/pagan. The Jew and the pagan are not even represented in such art. But icons are just one of the social practices that try to freeze the play of opposites—there are many more—such as advertising, social codes, taboos, conventions, categories, rituals, etc. But reality and language are not as simple and singular as icons with a central, exclusive image in their middle—they are more like ambiguous figures.

The interesting thing about such figures is that at first we see only one possibility. One possibility is "central" for a moment. For a moment the figure signifies two faces, but then, because the play of the system is not arrested, the other view dawns, and the same figure signifies a candle.

But suppose a group seizes power, a group called the Face-ists. (I have deliberately made this sound like "Fascists"). They might draw eyes on the faces. This would be an attempt to freeze or arrest the free play of differences. But— the figure, in reality, signifies *both* faces *and* a candle.

In such a situation, Candle-ists would be marginalized, repressed and even oppressed or persecuted. The image of the faces becomes the privileged member of the original pair. In other words a violent hierarchy is formed in which the centralized member of the pair, the face, becomes instituted as the Real and the Good.

Derrida says that all of Western thought behaves in the same way, forming pairs of binary opposites in which one member of the pair is privileged, freezing the play of the system, and marginalizing the other member of the pair.

25

Yes, but how does this apply to language, to literature, to reading?

**Deconstruction** is a tactic of decentering, a way of reading, which first makes us aware of the **centrality** of the central term.

Then it attempts to *subvert* the central term so that the marginalized term can become central.

The marginalized term temporarily overthrows the hierarchy.

Suppose you have a poem such as the following haiku:

*How mournfully the wind of autumn pines*
*Upon the mountainside as day declines.*

And suppose that for thousands of years the only correct way of reading the poem is to read "pines" as a verb—like pining for one's lost love.

O.K. But what about the other meaning. "Pines," in the context of the second line, can switch over and become a noun: "Pines upon the mountainside."

Yes, that's right. That would be the second move in deconstructing a piece of literature—to subvert the privileged term by revealing how the repressed, marginalized meaning can just as well be central.

But what good does that do? Doesn't this just institute a new center? Instead of pines the *verb* we have pines the *noun*. Or instead of Face-ists we now have Candle-ists in power?

Exactly. Derrida claims that deconstruction is a political practice, and that one must not pass over and neutralize this phase of subversion too quickly. For this phase **of reversal** is needed in order to subvert the original hierarchy of the first term over the second. But eventually, one must realize that this new hierarchy is equally unstable, and surrender to the complete free play of the binary opposites in a nonhierarchical way. Then you can see that both readings, and many others, are equally possible

YES! LIKE "PINES UPON THE MOUNTAIN SIGHED" (INSTEAD OF "MOUNTAIN SIDE")!

So you can see the possibilities. If the text were the *Communist Manifesto* or the Torah or the Koran or the Bible or the *Constitution*, you could deconstruct any fixed, authoritarian, dogmatic, or orthodox reading. Of course, such texts are much more complex than our haiku. They are more multifaceted, like the drawing below.

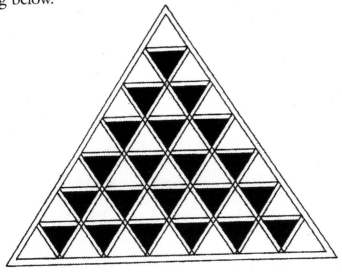

If you have a system of triangles such as this, then you will notice that if you stare at it, a series of configurations of triangles presents itself to your vision—one after the other. But each so-called *present* configuration, each group of triangles which seems to be momentarily *present*, has emerged out of a *prior* configuration and is already dissolving into a *future* configuration. And this *play* goes on endlessly. There is no central configuration that attempts to freeze the play of the system, no marginal one, no privileged one, no repressed one. According to Derrida all language and all texts are, when deconstructed, like this, and so is human thought, which is always made up of language. He says we should continuously attempt to see this *free play* in all our language and texts—which otherwise will tend toward fixity, institutionalization, centralization, totalitarianism. For out of *anxiety* we always feel a need to construct new centers, to associate ourselves with them, and marginalize those who are different from their central values.

I see, then. **Deconstruction** first focuses on the binary oppositions within a text—like man/woman. Next it shows how these opposites are related, how one is central, natural and privileged, the other ignored, repressed and marginalized. Next it temporarily undoes or subverts the hierarchy to make the text mean the opposite of what it originally appeared to mean. Then in the last step both terms of the opposition are seen dancing in a free play of non hierarchical, non-stable meanings.

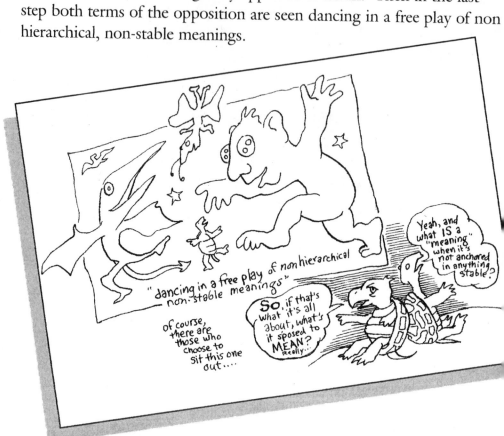

Yes, and now you can see why Derrida's lecture "Structure, Sign and the Play in the Discourse of the Human Sciences," caused such a stir. In this lecture Derrida asserted that all of Western thought since Plato, and even the work of scientists such as the contemporary French structural anthropologist Claude Lévi-Strauss, is infected with a yearning for a center. Derrida points out that this created a dilemma for Lévi-Strauss. After all, structuralists believe that all things have underlying structures. Every language, for instance, has a structure: its rules of grammar.

**RULE:**

In English we put the adjectives before the noun.
Big red apple.

**RULE:**

In French we put the adjectives after the noun.
*La pomme grosse et rouge.*

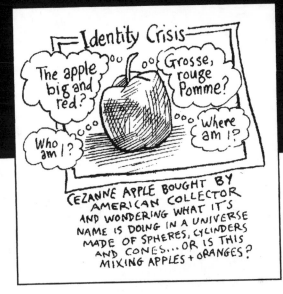

And you can make up millions of sentences based on each rule.

Lévi-Strauss felt that myths have a structure, too. In *The Raw and the Cooked*, the famous anthropologist set out to write a "grammar" of all Bororo myth—-but was forced to admit that he could find no central rules nor ever a central myth.

# OF GRAMMATOLOGY

Derrida's classic, *Of Grammatology*, is his most influential work in North America. It is the story of how—in the West—*speech* is central and natural and *writing* is marginal and unnatural.

**Q:** So this is the binary opposition? Speech/writing?

**A:** Yes, then Derrida shows how this **binary opposition** between speech and writing deconstructs itself.

**Q:** But who has said that writing is unnatural. Doesn't just about everyone write?

**A:** Well, yes. But for Derrida the entire Western tradition of thought—from the ancient philosophy of Plato to the Romantic philosophy of Jean Jacques Rousseau, and even the modern linguistics of Ferdinand de Saussure and the anthropology of Claude Lévi-Strauss—favors *speech*, the *spoken word* over *writing*, the *written word*.

*I CALL THIS BIAS LOGOCENTRISM.*

LÉVI-STRAUSS

**Q:** Logocentrism?

**A:** Yes. **Logocentrism** comes from *"logos,"* the Greek word that means word, truth, reason and law. The ancient Greeks thought of *logos* as a cosmic principle hidden deep within human beings, within speech and within the natural universe. If you are **Logocentric** you believe that **TRUTH** is the voice, the word, or the expression of a central, original and absolute **Cause** or **Origin**.

YEARNING FOR THE PRESENCE

THE ROOTS OF LOGOCENTRISM, OR THE NATIVITY OF THE LOGOS-ENTERISM, IN WHICH LUKE + JOHN +THE NIGHT BEFORE XMAS INTERPOLATE AND TURN INTO NUMINOUSITY

33

For instance, in the New Testament the Word is God.

## God is the Word.
# He is a God-Word,
# a Word-God,
# A Super-Word.

"In the beginning was the Word. And the Word was with God, and the Word was God,"

declares the Gospel of St. John. And as Western philosophy proceeded down through the centuries everything in the universe was seen as the effect of this one transcendent cause—this **transcendental signified.**

**Transcendental signified?** What's that?

Well, in order to know what a transcendental signified is, you must know what a signified is. You can see that the word "**sign**ified" contains the word "**sign**."

"sign" is a word. The sign "cow" is made up of the **sound** "cow"—which is the **signifier**—and the concept or **meaning** of "cow," which is the **signified**. (The actual animal is called the referent).

A **transcendental signified** is a meaning that lies beyond everything in the whole universe. After all, transcendent simply means that which is **beyond** everything else. For instance, the *logos*, the God-Word, supposedly lies beyond the entire universe. But though the God-Word dwells beyond the structure of the universe, the God-Word is thought of as centering and limiting the free play of the universe! He makes sure that cows never turn into cantelopes. He makes the rules. He makes good and evil. Yet, though he makes the rules, the God-Word is **beyond** the rules. He just sits down there—up beyond the rules, making the rules. Though He is beyond the structure of the world, He is its Center. He centers it.

During the long history of philosophy, other names have stood for an inner **transcendental signified**—names such as the Ideal, the World Spirit, Mind, the Divine Will, Consciousness, etc. (Such terms are usually capitalized). In Western philosophy these inner principles and the words or expressions which express them are central and involve a **metaphysics of presence**.

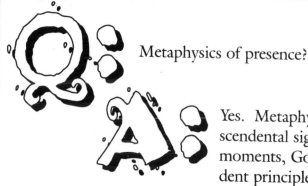

Metaphysics of presence?

Yes. Metaphysics is talk about transcendental signifieds, original moments, Golden Ages, transcendent principles, or an unarguable meaning for an utterance or text because it is divine. The metaphysics of presence is the notion that there is a transcendental signified, a God-Word that underlies all philosophical talk, and guarantees its meaning. It's like when I am talking with you now. It seems as if my talking with you is a present, direct expression of my thoughts, my emotions, even my spirit. My talk is how I **present** my thoughts and feelings to you. When I talk with you I seem to verbalize my true self. My words come directly from myself. They seem like a perfect one-to-one fit for my thoughts, feelings, intuitions—

$\mathcal{P}$resent TO
TO THEM.

Just like the uttered Word, the Logos, the Son, is believed by Christian theologians to be the perfect expression of God—

$\mathcal{P}$resent TO GOD.

Yes. Writing, however, seems less immediate. It seems more mechanical. If I write you a letter, and I am not there when you receive it, I feel that you might misread it. But I am always *present* to you if I am speaking to you, and my *presence* helps you understand me. So I would probably write to you only if I were **not** *present*.

WRITING, THEN, IS SEEN BY WESTERN THINKERS AS HAUNTED WITH **ABSENCE**.

Words, which are spoken in specific moments and places, are *present*.

YEARNING FOR PRESENCE
BUT FEELING ONLY THE CHILLY DRAFT
OF THE GREAT BLACK VOID
IN THE FACE OF ABSENCE

So the yearning for *presence* seems to be tied in with this favoring of language over writing, with logocentrism.

Absolutely. In fact Derrida says that the whole Western tradition, the whole history of logocentrism, is one vast **metaphysics of presence**.

"ALL THE NAMES RELATED TO FUNDAMENTALS, TO PRINCIPLES, OR TO THE CENTER HAVE ALWAYS DESIGNATED AN INVARIABLE PRESENCE." (SS; IN WD 278)

But **isn't** meaning immediately present when I speak to you? **Isn't** meaning more distant in writing, when I write to you?

That is precisely the central and seemingly natural assumption that Derrida unmasks or deconstructs in *Of Grammatology*. In his reading of a work by the Swiss linguist Ferdinand de Saussure, *Course in General Linguistics*, Derrida showed how Saussure sets up a binary opposition between speech and writing, and favors speech over writing.

It was in his *Course in General Linguistics* that Saussure defined language as made up of a system of signs.

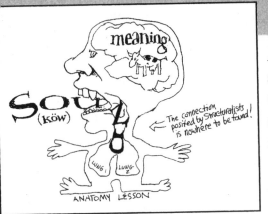

The connection posited by Structuralists is nowhere to be found!

ANATOMY LESSON

As we have seen, a linguistic **sign** like "cow" is made up of the **sound** "cow"—which is the **signifier**—and the **concept** or meaning of "cow," which is the **signified**. (The actual **animal** is called the **referent**).

OH DEAR I'M AFRAID YOU'RE NOT BEING AT ALL SIGNIFIED

STIX 'N' SCONES MAY BASTE MY PHONES BUT BLAMES WILL NEVER PERK ME

A CLEAR CASE OF MIXED SIGNALS

SOAP

Derrida's first argument with Saussure is that he regards the **signified**—the **meaning**—as more important than the **sound** "c-o-w," the **signifier**. For Saussure the tangible **sound** only gives us *access* to the intangible **meaning**. **Sound** is **outer**, meaning is **inner**.

**Q:** But doesn't that just repeat the logocentric Western notion that God-the-Father is the real inner meaning and Source and Essence of the Word, Christ?

**A:** Exactly. Derrida points out that just as the Western **metaphysics of presence** cherishes the idea of an *inner* Origin as a *presence within,* Saussure proclaims a *natural bond* between *inner meaning* and *outer sound.* Thus Saussure's linguistics, a *science* which is supposedly free of God talk, simply repeats the ancient *pre-scientific* assumptions of God talk.

Speech, according to Saussure, is natural and direct, immediatley intimate and *present* to thought and meaning. But Saussure degrades writing, asserting that it veils language, that it is not a guise for language but a disguise, that it is artificial, perverse, pathological, evil, degenerative and only used in the *absence* of speech.

Saussure also argues that just as speech is a way of representing inner meaning, writing is simply a means of representing speech. If speech is a *sign* of inner meaning—then writing, a *sign* of speech, is *twice* removed from inner meaning—a "sign of a sign."

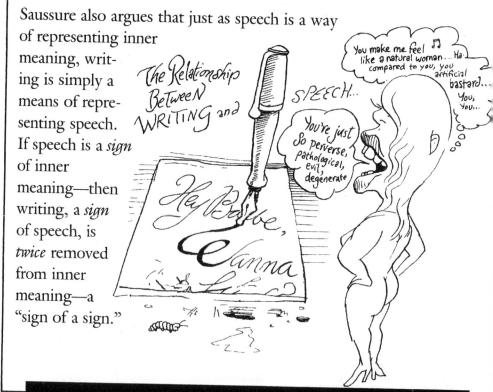

Therefore, concludes Saussure, the *sounds of speech, not writing,* should be the object of linguistics.

Well, the first stage is to see that Saussure privileges *speech* as *central* and natural because it is closer to inner meaning—just as the Logos, the Word and the Son are close to God. He marginalizes *writing* as perverted and evil. All that is needed for the second stage is a deconstructive reversal, revealing how *writing* can be seen as *central* in Saussure's own text.

And that's what Derrida unravels next. He reminds us how, on the one hand, Saussure says there is a *natural bond* between *sound* (the signifier) "c-o-w" and *meaning* (the signified) "cow"—as if meaning (the signified) depended upon some sort of natural correspondence with the sound c-o-w.

But Saussure also said that the *link* between the (sound) *signifier* "c-o-w," and its *signified meaning* is just due to chance. In French one says "vache," in Swahili one says "ng'ombe jike," in Arabic "baqara," in Japanese "meushi" to signify "cow.". *So there is nothing essential in the sound "c-o-w" that relates it to its meaning*.

In fact on the level of sound, "c-o-w" gains its identity only because it is slightly *different* from "Mao" which is only slightly *different* from "sow" which is only slightly different from "bough" which is only slightly *different* from "bout!"

The *sound* "cow," in other words, depends upon its ***difference*** from these ***other*** sounds, these ***other*** signifiers—to distinguish itself from them.

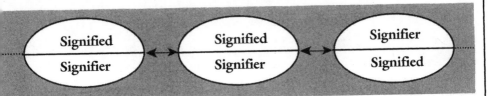

 So the (horizontal) *difference* between *sound* and *sound* is what shapes the sounds of language, not some vertical, intimate correspondence between *sound* and *meaning*.

 Yes. There is only this vast interwoven system of differences. A sound is what it is only because it differs from other sounds in the same language. It gains its being through being different from them.

Similarly, on the level of *meaning*, the **concept** "cow," the *signified*, has no *meaning* in-and-of-itself. Our *concepts* distinguish themselves only through their ***difference*** from other *concepts*. The concept "boat" gains its identity by being different from the concept of "ship" or "yawl."

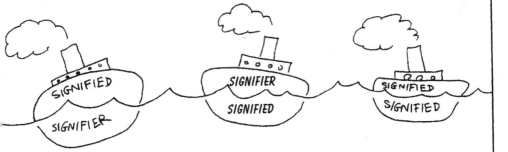

 So on the level of the **concept**, the signified, also there is only a system of differences.

And there is no stable foundation to the system of differences which language is. For instance if you didn't **know** English, and wanted to know what a cow is, you would have to look up "cow" in the dictionary. But under the entry "cow," instead of finding a **meaning** that would satisfy your search for a meaning, since you don't know English, you would only find a bunch of other **sounds**:

COW: N. THE MATURE FEMALE OF DOMESTIC CATTLE, OR OF VARIOUS OTHER ANIMALS, AS THE WHALE, ELEPHANT, ETC.

COWS THIS WAY PLEASE

MEANING

AN ENDLESS CHAIN THAT NEVER REACHES MEANING

 I see! But in order to know the meaning of the sounds "cattle," "whale," and "elephant," you would have to look up their meanings, their signifieds, but you would find only more lists of signifiers, more sounds! A whale is a large mammal that lives in the sea, but then what is a mammal, what is a sea?

 Yes! So you never arrive at a *stable signified, a stable meaning* that is capable of providing a foundation for the entire system in meaning! Because every potential *meaning* turns out to be just another **sound**, searching for yet another potential **meaning**. You never reach **meaning**—there is only an endless chain of sounds.

It's just like our system of triangles:

here is no configuration of triangles which can ground the system, make it stable. Each wave of triangles that seems to become present has risen from a past wave and is dissolving into a future wave. Just look nd you will see.

Then Derrida points out that Saussure, in trying to describe how *language* is just a vast tissue of differences, must employ a graphic system—*writing*—as an example. For writing is purely just a play of differences:

For instance, the marks **B**, **A**, **d** mean nothing in-and-of themselves. They have no essential features. They gain their identity only through their difference from other elements in their system:

```
    12
A   B   C
    14
```

```
    T
C   A   T
    E
```

```
        r
        i
bicycle
        e
```

Thus, Saussure says that language is a system of differences with no stable, "positive" elements, no unchanging linguistic atoms that might provide a foundation for language.

But if language, made up of sound and meaning, is just a play of differences, and if the relationship between the *sound* C-O-W and its *meaning* changes from language to language, then how can Saussure still claim that there is a *natural bond* between sound and meaning? How can he privilege speech as the natural presence of meaning, and trash writing as evil and absent from meaning? After all, as Saussure himself explains, both the *meanings* and *sounds* of speech are systems of difference just like writing.

The sound C-O-W is different from "bough" or "wow." And the meaning "cow" is different from "horse." It is the play of difference that makes the sounds and meanings. And this play of difference in speaking is just like the play of difference in writing. For in writing an "r" means nothing in itself, but is what it is because it is different from "t" or "l." So it could be said that speaking is like a form of writing!

That's right. And this is the deconstructive reversal—to **invert** the hierarchy that favors **speech** as natural and central and to reveal how **writing**, which had been seen as perverted, pathological and derivative, can be central and not marginal.

But Derrida does not stop at that. For to do so would be to just replace speech with writing. What he does next is to show that **neither** the word "speech" **nor** the word "writing" is adequate to describe the more abstract play of differences which they both are; **both speech and writing are just a play of difference.**

So Derrida is not simply reversing the hierarchy—making writing central and speech marginal. What he does next is to put **both** terms, writing **and** speaking, **under erasure**, or in French *sous rature*!

*SOUS RATURE! NOW YOU'RE LOSING ME!*

SOUS RATURE

46

Derrida indicates that concepts are under erasure by drawing an "X" through them. To put a binary opposition **under erasure** you write the words, but then mark a big black "X" over them, thus:

spe~~e~~ch

wri~~ti~~ng

It is a device Derrida borrowed from the philosopher Martin Heidegger, and it simply means that **both** "speech" and "writing" are <u>inadequate</u> to describe the more general **play of differences** common to both. But in discussing the matter,

he simply can not do without them. So they **must** be used. And putting them *under erasure* allows Derrida to have his cake and eat it too, so to speak. It allows him to use a word or concept and simultaneously indicate its highly inadequate nature.

Yes, and Derrida's next step, then, is to invent an expression which shows that *speaking* and *writing* are just the *spoken* and *written* forms of the play of difference, a non-existent form of "writing" he calls arche-writing.

**Q:** Non-existent?

**A:** Yes. **Arche-writing** is not merely writing on a page, graphic marks, or sounds. It is not the Roman alphabet. It is not any kind of "marking" that can be made with the voice, with pictures, with hieroglyphics, with cunieforms, with Chinese characters, with choreography, with musical notation, with the forms of sculpture in space, which can be marked with an awl on oak, with lips on breasts, with pen on paper, with fingers on sand, with hands on clay, by the contrast of light and shadow on film. **Arche-writing** is not a thing. It is the pure possibility of contrast, of difference. **Arche-writing** makes possible the *play* of differences. *It does not exist as a thing*, yet makes all these possible. **Arche-writing** is not a concept, nor even a word which can be defined. It is like the play of the triangles, the possibility of differing that underlies the play. And grammatology is the science of **arche-writing**.

Having displayed how Saussure's argument about the centrality of speech deconstructs itself, Derrida proceeds to make the same sorts of moves on the 18th century French philosopher Jean Jacques Rousseau, the father of French Romanticism.

In *Discourse on the Sciences and the Arts*, *Discourse on the Origin and Bases of Inequality*, and *Confessions*, Rousseau reacted against the view of his contemporaries that progress in the arts and sciences will make human beings happy. Instead, he argued that civilization and learning corrupt human nature. He celebrated the "original," "natural," uncivilized man, the "noble savage" who was innocent of writing, private property and the powerful institutions of the political state.

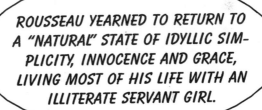

ROUSSEAU YEARNED TO RETURN TO A "NATURAL" STATE OF IDYLLIC SIMPLICITY, INNOCENCE AND GRACE, LIVING MOST OF HIS LIFE WITH AN ILLITERATE SERVANT GIRL.

Rousseau's writings depend upon a **binary opposition** between *nature* and *culture*. Nature is good, original, virtuous, noble, and present. **Culture** is corrupt, degenerate, a "*supplement*" to nature's fullness of presence.

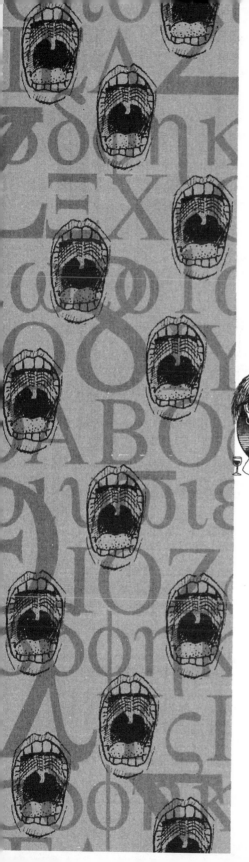

Rousseau also feels that writing is per verse—a product of civilization, a dangerous **supplement** to natural speech. He argues that in small-scale, organic, living communities the face-to-face presence of speech had eventually given way to civilization, to inequalities of power and economics, and to the loss of the ability to speak one-on-one.

For Rousseau it is writing that has intruded upon the idyllic communal peace and grace of the one-to-one intimacy of natural speaking societies.

But isn't Rousseau's dream of an idyllic, intimate, primitive, speaking community simply th social and political equivalent of logocentrism and the metaphysics of presence? Isn't he just yearning for the full presence of speech and distrusting writing?

He is. And Derrida's task, then, is to demonstrate how Rousseau's writings deconstruct themselves.

Well, for one thing, they *are writings*, aren't they. I mean, Rousseau is not present to us. He is absent. He is not speaking, We know him only through his writing, which he must depend on to communicate his thought to us.

That is his predicament. And he recognizes it. In his *Confessions*, Rousseau, writing in a candid, confessional mode, realizes that even though writing is artificial and decadent, he *is* a writer. He realizes that he must rely upon writing to make his own most intimate thoughts and feelings known, *even to himself*. And that's not all. He also confesses that when writing down the history of his life and emotions, that he feels tempted to embellish, to fictionalize, to dress up the original, natural truth.

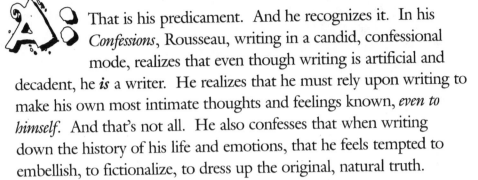

THUS, HE CONCLUDES THAT WRITING IS A DANGEROUS **SUPPLEMENT** TO SPEECH.

Derrida seizes upon the fact that *suppléer*, supplement, in French, can mean not only
1) *to supplement*, to add on to—but also
2) *to take the place of*, to substitute for.

So **supplement** is paradoxical, it can mean **adding something on to something already complete in itself,** or **adding on something to complete a thing**.

So it is like an ambigram.

Yes. And for Rousseau, writing is both something that is added on to speech, which is supposedly already complete and full presence—and it is something which makes speech complete. But speech is obviously **not** complete if it needs writing to supplement it. It is **not** full of presence. It **must** contain absence.

And then Derrida shows that for Rousseau *all his human activities* invo this play of presence/absence.

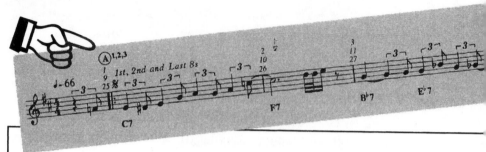

For instance, Rousseau writes that melody—the pure, spontaneous impulse to sing—is *central*, because it is so present to the natural voice.

Harmony, on the other hand—the arrangement of multiple voices in concert—is unnatural. After all it depends upon notation, which is a form of writing. Rousseau argues that as civilization becomes more complex, more abstract, written **harmonies** replace the innocent grace of natural speech-song—**melody**.

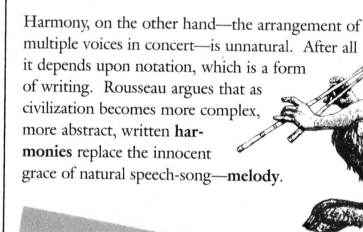

But Derrida shows how Rousseau's argument deconstructs itself. Rousseau writes that melody "has its principle in harmony, since it is an harmonic analysis that gives degrees of the scale, and the chords of the mode, and the laws of modulation, the only elements of singing."

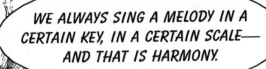

WE ALWAYS SING A MELODY IN A CERTAIN KEY, IN A CERTAIN SCALE— AND THAT IS HARMONY.

 So, the pure, pristine *melody* is always already a form of its dangerous *supplement—harmony*!

 Rousseau also writes of how the "secret vice," masturbation, is a dangerous *supplement—* for it substitutes or adds a perverse, solitary and weakening pleasure to the normal, natural presence of erotic experience with a lover. The masturbator has fantasies about absent beauties with his imagination, supplementing them for the real thing.

And both sex and masturbation, realizes Rousseau, may be just a substitute for his foster-mother, his original object of desire. Thus the masturbator, the fantasist, is engaged in an endless quest. For his fantasies—and even his lovers—can never replace the full presence he enjoyed with his foster-mother.

But isn't that just another form of the yearning for full presence all over again? Just another example of what Derrida calls the metaphysics of presence?

Yes. And what Derrida reveals is that throughout the *Confessions*, Rousseau relies upon the dangerous *supplement*, fantasy—because he admits that at the very core of "natural" sexual desire—there is *lack, absence*. Rousseau admits that his "natural" erotic experiences with women have never been as passionate, as exciting and fulfilling, as his erotic dreams and daytime fantasies. Sex cannot live up to fantasy.

**NEITHER CAN LIVE UP TO THE FULLNESS OF PRESENCE HE ONCE FELT WITH HIS FOSTER-MOTHER.**

So like speech and melody, the presence of sex is always, already inhabited by a certain, lack, by an absence, which then must be filled in with a dangerous supplement—fantasy.

Yes. Rousseau favors speech, melody, nature and sex. But then Derrida notices how Rousseau finds a dangerous *supplement* in all of these—in harmony, in writing, in civilization and in fantasy or masturbation—regarding all these *supplements* as marginal.

| **central** | **marginal** |
| --- | --- |
| melody | harmony |
| speech | writing |
| nature | civilization |
| sex | fantasy/masturbation |

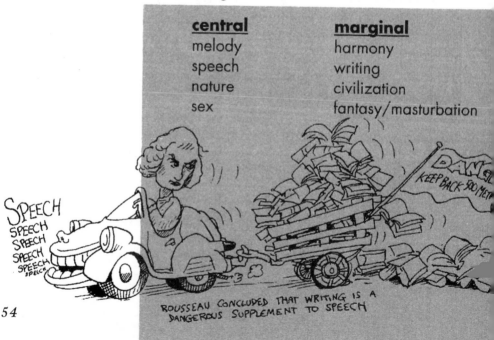

SPEECH SPEECH SPEECH SPEECH SPEECH SPEECH

ROUSSEAU CONCLUDED THAT WRITING IS A DANGEROUS SUPPLEMENT TO SPEECH

54

BUT IF SOMETHING NEEDS A **SUP-PLEMENT,** THERE MUST BE SOMETHING **LACKING** IN IT IN THE FIRST PLACE—THERE MUST ALWAYS ALREADY BE **ABSENCE** IN IT.

YES. AND THIS IS HOW DERRIDA BRINGS ABOUT THE DECONSTRUCTIVE REVERSAL OR INVERSION, SHOWING HOW THE MARGINALIZED TERMS CAN BE CENTRAL.

Yes, it seems that in everything that Rousseau found fullness of *presence*, there was, in Derrida's view, always already an *original* lack, and *absence* at work. Yet, Rousseau's whole argument depends upon maintaining that melody, speech, etc, are full.

Yes, so Derrida shakes up the stability of these pairs of binary opposites, by playing upon the double meaning of the term *supplement*. For again, in French it can mean to *add something on to* a thing already complete in itself, or to *complete* a thing by adding on to it. *Supplement*, then, cannot be defined simply. Like the ambigraph of the faces and the candles, it is two things at once.

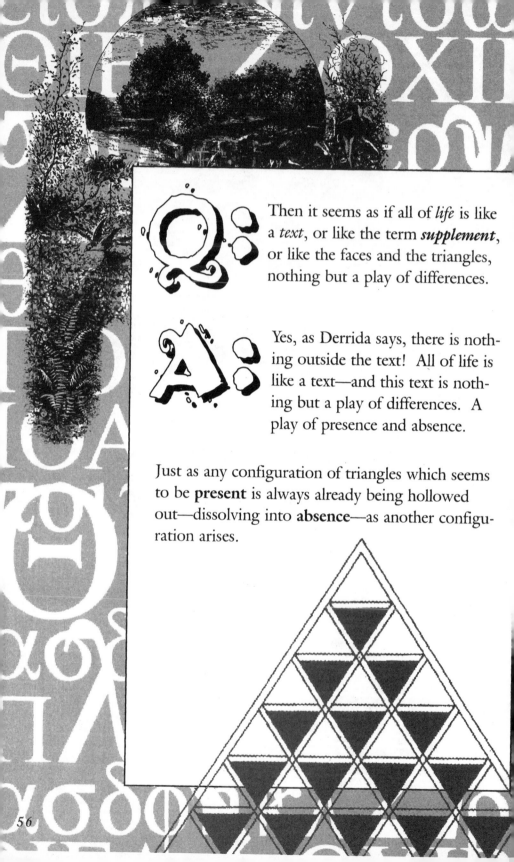

**Q:** Then it seems as if all of *life* is like a *text*, or like the term **supplement**, or like the faces and the triangles, nothing but a play of differences.

**A:** Yes, as Derrida says, there is nothing outside the text! All of life is like a text—and this text is nothing but a play of differences. A play of presence and absence.

Just as any configuration of triangles which seems to be **present** is always already being hollowed out—dissolving into **absence**—as another configuration arises.

Derrida also turns his attention to the French anthropologist Claude Lévi-Strauss, for it was Lévi-Strauss who applied Saussure's structural linguistics to the study of anthropology in general and myth in particular.

Both Rousseau and Lévi-Strauss base all their arguments on the binary opposition between **nature** and **culture**.

NATURE IS INNOCENT, PURE AND NATURAL.

CULTURE IS CORRUPTING, PERVERSE.

Both Rousseau and Lévi-Strauss favor *nature* over *culture*. Both long for a lost innocence. And both see writing as a perverse *supplement* to natural speech.

The Natural Innocence and Fullness of Speech

The Corrupt, Perverse and Corrupting Influence of WRITING

MY BABY DONE GONE AND LEFT ME...

BUT IN SPEECH, THERE IS ALWAYS ALREADY ABSENCE!

Derrida, however, delights in showing how Rousseau's dream of purity, innocence and presence shows up even in a modern science like anthropology. The text Derrida deconstructs here is Lévi-Straus's "The Writing Lesson," a chapter in his book *Tristes Tropiques* (*Sad Tropics*).

*Tristes Tropiques* is the story of Lévi-Strauss's anthropological field work in the wilds of Brazil. There he finds the Nambikwara, a tribe in which he sees the perfect example of primitive naturalness. In fact, in his role as anthropologist, Lévi-Strauss feels guilty—like a voyeur, an alien "civilized" man who can only corrupt the pure communal innocence of this primitive culture which knows no writing—only speaking. Lévi-Strauss admires their closeness to nature, their open, communal sexuality, their way of knowing through myth rather than through science.

When he is writing in his notebook, some of the Nambikwara began to imitate him, making various wavy lines. This is unusual, thinks Lévi-Strauss, because the Nambikwara neither write nor draw. The closest they come to either is a few dots and zigzags they make on their gourds.

But then Lévi-Strauss notices that the leader of the tribe immediately grasps the utility of writing—how it can be used to reinforce his own power, and to maintain the unequal distribution of goods in his own favor. This leader is able to convince his followers that he knows how to write and therefore has power.

IT MUST BE POINTED OUT THAT THIS LEADER HAS THREE BEAUTIFUL WIVES, AS THE LEADERS OF THE NAMBIKWARA GET ANYTHING THEY WANT.

And this, as Derrida is quick to point out, is where Lévi-Strauss's argument begins to deconstruct itself. For the Nambikwara are always already engaged in a system of differences—of inequalities in power and the distribution of "goods." Though the members of the tribe cannot write in the usual sense, Derrida illustrates how the tribe's unequal relations are in fact already indicated and maintained by various taboos, myths, codes and customs which are, in effect, a form of marking, of "writing" without an alphabet. So Lévi-Strauss's fantasy of the Nambikwara as innocent and pure, as free from writing and the corrupting influences of civilization, is just a fantasy. It only shows that he yearns for a kind of logocentric presence.

# DISSEMINATION

Another of Derrida's influential books in the United States is what most people would call a collection of three essays. It is entitled *Dissemination*. The first problem one notices, however, is that this book is a kind of non-book. Its preface refuses to be a preface. Its three essays refuse to be a collection or to present a thesis in the customary manner.

IN FACT DERRIDA'S STYLE IS MORE OF A **PERFORMANCE**, A SONG AND DANCE, A MIME SHOW, THAN AN ARGUMENT.

We must go against the spirit of this performance in trying to extract "its meaning." At the time he wrote *Dissemination*, Derrida was associated with the ultra-left, avant-garde Parisian journal *Tel Quel*, a publication flirting with how a word, a poem, or language in general, can mean many things at once. Members of the *Tel Quel* group experimented with automatic writing, devoting themselves to an entire gang of surrealists, and to Mao and Mallarmé besides.

Each of the essays in *Dissemination* is divided into two parts, and each concerns itself with how the illusion of presence is presented or represented.

# DISSEMINATION 1

## PLATO'Z PHARMACY

The first "essay," "Plato's Pharmacy," criticizes the very foundations of Western philosophy. In it, Plato's put-down of writing as second-hand and illusory, dead, and full of nothing but fake wisdom, is deconstructed by his contradictory statement that writing is the very voice of Truth and Being written in the very soul.

# ROOTS OF WESTERN CIVILIZATION

The rite of the scapegoat or ***pharmakos*** was a civil purification ritual. Ancient Grecian cities fed and housed, at public expense, a group of wild, ugly, deformed human beings solely for the purpose of sacrifice. Then, when flood, famine, pestilence or any other bane seized a city, the citizens selected the most unattractive of these, led him out of the city, positioned him in the place of sacrifice, fed him with their own hands—barley cakes and figs—then struck him with leeks, wild figs and other wild plants, the death spasm arriving only as the last in a series of throes brought on by a frenzied pounding of his penis and scrotum with squills—a bulbous herb. Then they ignited a fire fed with the wood of wild trees, offered the corpse unto the flames, and finally scattered the ashes to the four winds and tossing seas. Thus the city was purified.

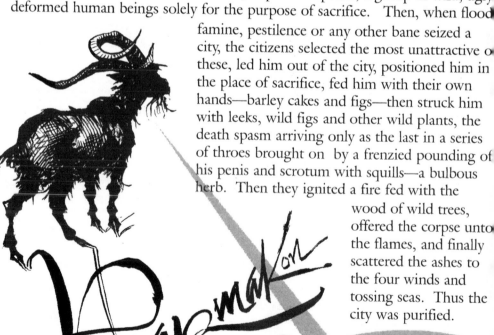

**SUCH WAS THE FATE OF THE SCAPEGOAT IN ANCIENT GREECE**

IN "PLATO'S PHARMACY," DERRIDA ARGUES THAT THE GREEK PHILOSOPHER SOCRATES BECAME SOMETHING OF A SCAPEGOAT AND THAT, IN A SENSE, SO DID **WRITING**.

have said that Derrida's "essay" has no eme. But the theme of the essay would ve been, if there would have been one, e play of **textuality**.

 Textuality?  Yes. **Textuality** is realizing **how** a text means rather than **what** it means. It is the realization that a text is made up of **words**, and that **words** can mean different things.

We recognize **textuality** when we realize that the word "pines" in the text:

*How mournfully the wind of Autumn pines Upon the mountainside as day declines.*

can have different meanings, and that the meaning of the text is never **settled** but always already **open** to the **play** of **textuality**, the play of "pines."

63

And **textuality**, the play of differences in writing, **in** and **between** books, poems, phrases, verses, ideograms, hieroglyphics, is an **irresistible** force. It cannot be repressed. This *play* is always already a fertile, potent ejaculation of meanings, a swarming of meanings, a **dissemination** or dispersal of meanings.

> DERRIDA EXPLOITS THE FACT THAT THE WORD DISSEMINATION SOUNDS AS IF IT CONTAINS THE WORD SEME (MEANING) AND SEMEN.

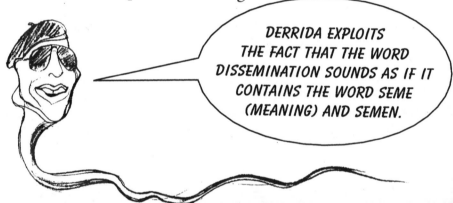

Yet, textuality is constantly called a villain, a fatal poison. Like the scapegoat who must be expelled from the very heart of the city, textuality, the play of meanings, must be violently ejected from nearness to the *logos*, the fixed, orthodox, rational, paternal, authoritative, spoken Word and the all-knowing Light of Truth of which this Word is the living body.

"PLATO'S PHARMACY" IS DERRIDA'S UNIQUE READING OF THE <u>PHAEDRUS</u>, ONE OF THE SOCRATIC DIALOGUES WHICH WAS WRITTEN DOWN BY PLATO, A STUDENT OF SOCRATES.
BECAUSE SOCRATES AND PLATO ARE SEMINAL, THE FATHERS OF MEANING IN WESTERN THOUGHT, DERRIDA DISSEMINATES THEM.

Derrida's method is twofold:

**1)** first he offers a reading of the *Phaedrus* as Plato would have us read it, then

**2)** his second reading does not embroider upon the dialogue so much as look closely at how the dialogue is woven together like a tapestry. He finds a loose thread, and then follows that thread to reveal how Plato's own argument unravels itself. The thread Derrida follows concerns *writing*, especially as Plato and Socrates use it in the binary opposition *speaking/writing*. And Plato calls writing a *pharmakon*.

*Pharmakon*? What does that mean?

Well, it has many meanings, but for now, just know that it means *poison*, *drug*, or *allurement*, because that is how Plato or Socrates would have us view writing.

The dialogue opens as Socrates and his friend Phaedrus are driven by the oppressive heat out of the city into the countryside. There they follow the river Ilissus, the fresh summer air filled with sweetness and the resounding song of the cicadas. It is here that the thread Derrida is following—*pharmakon*—and words related to it—first makes its appearance.

hen Phaedrus speaks, he speaks in the language of *mythos*, of myth:

"'Isn't this 'the spot,' asks Phaedrus, where Boreas, according to tradition, carried off Orithyia? This riverbank, the diaphanous purity of these waters, must have welcomed the young virgins, or even drawn them like a spell, inciting them to play here.'" (D 69)

ocrates offers a rational reply— peaking in the language of *logos*, **f reason**—saying that it was real- while playing with another aiden named **Pharmacia** that e *wind* swept the young virgin to the abyss. The **myth** that he was seized and raped by Boreas is only a **myth**, and not o be taken seriously.

The point that Derrida makes is that through her games **Pharmacia** has violated a virginal purity, an unpenetrated interior. And

**Pharmacia**, Derrida tells us, means, among other things, the administration of the *pharmakon*: the **drug**—the **medicine**—the **poison**.

**B**ut not only has the virgin been seduced away from her normal paths as if by a drug, so has Socrates (and Derrida). For Socrates is seduced not only by the beauty of the natural surroundings, but also by the *written* text of a speech Phaedrus is carrying beneath his robe. Derrida claims that a spoken speech, unadorned and naked, spoken in the presence of Socrates, would not have seduced him, or anyone: "Only words that are deferred, reserved, enveloped, rolled up, words that force one to wait for them in the form and under cover of a solid object, letting themselves be desired for the space of a walk, only hidden letters can thus get Socrates moving" (D 71). And, indeed, Socrates refers to the **written** speech as a *pharmakon*, an allurement, a dangerous *drug*.

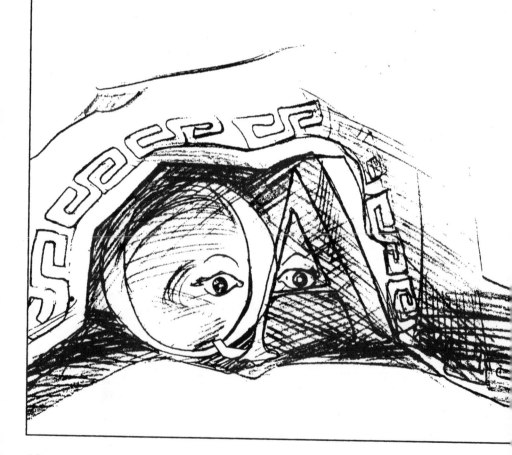

But then, what is this **writing**, this *pharmakon*, this seductive lure, this dangerous drug?

Well, you see, you are trying to make **pharmakon** into a concept, to hook it into a logocentric present, to make it full of meaning, full of presence in the present, now! But Derrida would say that we would have to put off the answer to that, indefinitely, for we can **never** really say what *pharmakon* "is!"

DERRIDA'S POINT IS THAT SOCRATES (AND PLATO) DO ATTEMPT TO ILLUSTRATE WHAT **PHARMAKON** MEANS BY INSISTING, AT CERTAIN POINTS, ON ONLY ONE OF ITS MANY MEANINGS.

Though he has just mocked **myth**, Socrates is going to use a **myth** to illustrate the "truth" about writing—even though he regards both **myth** and writing as merely "**repeating without knowing**." He feels that though **myths** are perhaps useful for teaching stupid lessons to simpletons, they can never lead to truth—to enlightenment. In fact the illumined *logos* pervading the *well-reasoned arguments* Socrates uses to unsettle various sophists, poets, flim-flam artists and others stands in sharp contrast to the use of *myth*—which is only the empty repetition of fabulous stories which have been handed down for ages. So **myth**, like writing, is not **real** thinking but *merely repeating without knowing*.

69

**Q:** Well, what is the myth?

**A:** The **myth** Socrates uses to illustrate the truth about wri[t]ing is the **myth** of Theuth.

**Q:** Theuth?

**A:** Yes, Theuth is the Greek nam[e] for the Egyptian god of Thot[h,] god of the occult sciences: of magic, of alchemy, of astrolog[y,] of incantations for calming the seas, of dice and draughts—and also the god [of] numbers, of medicine and of *writing*. Thoth is the son of the god-King an[d] Sun-God Ammon Ra—the Hidden Sun. Derrida points out that, in a w[ay] Thoth replaces or substitutes for Ra, representing him through speech and writing.

Very well, I heard that in Egypt there lived one of the old gods of that country, the one whose sacred bird is called the ibis; and the name of the divinity was Theuth. It was he who first invented numbers and calculation, geometry and astronomy, not to speak of draughts and dice, and above all writing. Now the King of all Egypt at that time was Thamus. Theuth came to him and exhibited his arts and declared that they ought to be given to the other Egyptians. And Thamus questioned him about the usefulness of each one; and as Theuth enumerated, the King blamed or praised what he thought were the good or bad points in the explanation. But when it came to writing; Theuth said, "This discipline, my King, will make the Egyptians wiser and will improve their memories: my invention is a recipe (*pharmakon*) for both memory and wisdom."
[paraphrase of (D 75)]

But the king said, "Theuth, my master of arts, to one man it is given to create the elements of an art, to another to judge the extent of harm and usefulness it will have for those who are going to employ it. And now, since you are father of written letters, your paternal goodwill has led you to pronounce the very opposite of what is their real power. The fact is that this invention will produce forgetfulness in the souls of those who have learned it because they will not need to exercise their memories, being able to rely on what is written, using the stimulus of external marks that are alien to themselves rather than, from within, their own unaided powers to call things to mind. So it's not a remedy for memory, but for reminding, that you have discovered. And as for wisdom, you're equipping your pupils with only a semblance of it, not with truth. Thanks to you and your invention, your pupils will be widely read without benefit of a teacher's instruction; in consequence, they'll entertain the delusion that they have wide knowledge, while they are, in fact, for the most part incapable of real judgement. They will also be difficult to get on with since they will be men filled with the conceit of wisdom, not men of wisdom."
[paraphrase of (D 102)]

Derrida shows that the mythology of Thoth or Theuth is like a tapestry woven of these threads of **binary opposites**. The privileged, favored, "good" member of each pair, the "teacher's pet," is on the left. The "dunce" is on the right.

Ra/Thoth (Teuth)
speech/writing
*logos/mythos*
King/subject
inside/outside
son/orphan, bastard son
sun/moon
life/death
good kind of memory/evil memory

But so is Socrates' retelling of the myth woven of a series of binary opposites, and so is the dialogue:

**speech / writing**
**philosopher / sophist**
**citizen / scapegoat**
**good seed / bad seed**

The "good" member of each pair is like the part of the thread that shows in the tapestry. While the marginalized member is like the part of the thread that lies below the surface of the design, repressed.

73

NOW, REMEMBER, SOCRATES HAS SAID THAT WRITING IS LIKE MYTHOS. BUT WRITING ALSO SHARES KINSHIP WITH ALL THE MARGINALIZED MEMBERS IN THE LIST OF BINARY OPPOSITES. WRITING IS AKIN TO EVIL MEMORY, TO A BASTARD, TO BAD SEED, TO A SOPHIST AND TO A SCAPEGOAT. THEY ARE ALL PHARMAKONS—POISONS.

Writing, for instance is like the evil kind of memory.

But how is writing like evil memory?

 For Socrates, the *good* kind of memory is the *re-cognition* of the Ideal Forms, the Spiritual Truths which illumine the soul but which we, caught up in the shadows of mere sensory perception, have forgotten. This kind of memory is unfolded by *logos*, by the rational method of the Socratic dialogue.

he evil kind of memory is mere *reminding*—learning something "by
eart." And it is *writing*, according to Socrates and Plato and the
ing, that encourages mere *reminding*.

LIKE, I COULD **WRITE** DOWN
YOUR PHONE NUMBER TO
**REMIND** ME OF IT.

Not a chance! But how is writing
like an orphan and a bastard son?

Because *logos*—Speech and Truth—is the good, legitimate
son. For just as when I am speaking to you now, I can be
said to be the *originator* and *father* of my speech—*logos*,
Reason and Speech, is like a *good* son who enjoys the presence
of a living father—"his" Origin.

WRITING, ON THE OTHER HAND, IS LIKE
AN ORPHAN OR BASTARD SON, BECAUSE
IT HAS NO INTIMATE CONTACT WITH
ANY PATERNAL, LIVING ORIGIN.

**Q:** Well, then, how is writing like bad seed?

**A:** Socrates compares writing to bad, sterile seed and speech to good, fertile seed or semen. Just as *writing outside*, away from the *logos* and its Origin—bad seed or semen is that which is scattered wastefully **outside**, like the seeds that produce mere flowers.

> SPEECH, THOUGH, IS LIKE FRUIT-BEARING SEEDS.

Socrates also associates the wasteful outpouring of sperm with the masks, allusions, play, frivolities, flirtations, peversities and pleasures of games and festivals. For Socrates writing is similarly wasteful, infertile, mere *dissemination*—without meaning or produce. Like speech, fertile seed, on the other hand, is the product of prudent agriculture; it is potent—*insemination*.

Similarly, the myth identifies speech with life and the King because it is in contact with the living father, the living voice. Thoth, the god of writing, the son, however, is aligned with the dead letter, with hieroglyphics, with the breathless, lifeless signifier.

**Q:**

hen how is riting like a ophist?

**A:**

ocrates distinguish-  between truly ise men and fake, elf-proclaimed wise en who, like writ-ng and myth, mere-repeat without nowing—they erely imitate. Like riting and myth—ophists, fake wise en—in order to eep their simple-minded clients appy, feed them pablum—not giving hem true remem-brance of the Ideal forms, but mere memorials. Just as vriting—graphic marks, hieroglyphics, cuneiforms, alpha-bets—can simply be repeated mechanical-ly, sophists or fake wise men repeat genealogies, histo-ries, myths, fables, etc, to keep their clients happy. They merely repeat with-out knowing.

It is no easy task to distinguish between a true wise guy and a mere goodfella...

FIRST WE MUST UNDERSTAND WHY WRITING IS LIKE A SOPHIST, RIGHT?

Are any of these guys for real?

What's real?

WISE GUY

**Q:** Then how is writing like a scapegoat?

**A:** Writing is like a scapegoat because it is pushed to the outside—far from the vicinity of logos and truth. The scape-goat or *pharmakos* is led out of the city, fed, flogged on the genitals with wild plants until death, and then burned.

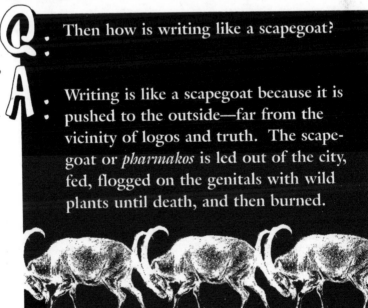

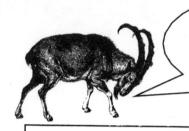

BUT REMEMBER, BOTH THE MYTH THAT SOCRATES USES TO TELL OF THE EVIL, THE POISON, THE **PHARMAKON** OF WRITING, OF SOPHISTS, OF MYTH, OF BAD MEMORY, ETC.—**AND** SOCRATIC DIALOGUE ARE LIKE TAPESTRIES WOVEN OF BINARY OPPOSITES.

So when Derrida unravels a single binary opposition—a single loose thread—that of writing as *pharmakon*—*the whole tapestry unravels.* For *pharmakon* is **not** simply a *poison*.

IT CAN ALSO MEAN THE EXACT OPPOSITE—A HEALING REMEDY OR MEDICINE!!!

AND IT CAN ALSO MEAN A POTION, AN ENCHANTMENT OR PHILTER, A CHARM OR SPELL, ETC.

And if this is the case, if *pharmakon* can have many meanings, then it is always already in the process of reversing and unraveling the entire tapestry of woven binary opposites it is supposed to be upholding. It is always already unweaving the texture of the seeming design of the dialogue it has woven. Once this happens, the dialogue's instability, movement and play cannot be stopped or frozen, for this instability of *pharmakon* puts the play of difference into play.

Plato, of course, attempts to **stop** this play, to repress the play of differences, by insisting on one meaning. But if the *pharmakon*, writing, can be *both* a poison *and* a remedy, a medicine, a philter, etc., then it has no *fixed* meaning. And then **all** the marginalized terms: evil memory, bastard, son, Theuth, sophist, death, outside, bad seed and scapegoat—which are also called *pharmakon*, and which are interwoven with writing, have no fixed meanings either!

AND THE PRISTINE, VIRGINAL PURITY OF THE LOGOS, OF SPEECH, OF THE INTERIOR OF THE CITY, CAN NO LONGER BE MAINTAINED.

Once the meanings of *pharmakon* begin to play within the fabric of Plato's dialogue, its seemingly seamless logic disseminates, begins to unravel, and there is no seemly way to arrest the play of differences. One can never draw a final dividing line or regulate the play between *poison* and *remedy*, *inner* and *outer*, *good memory* and *bad memory*, *philosopher* and *sophist*, etc.

Because all the *privileged* terms of the binary opposites are *defined* in terms of *marginalized* terms! *Truth*, as Socrates himself says, is a *kind of good "writing"* in the soul. So *writing*, which had been pushed to the outside, marginalized, is now suddenly seen to be in the very heart of the interior.

 And Derrida explains how this binary opposition between inner and outer is overthrown, how the virginal purity of the "inner" is always already penetrated by the "outer."

 Yes, Socrates uses a marginalized term "myth" (that which repeats without knowing) to tell the *truth* or *logos* about *writing* (that which repeats without knowing). So the central term, truth or *logos,* is "penetrated" by myth.

 Yes, and the virginal purity of *true wisdom* is always already infected from within by fake wisdom of the *sophists*, for Derrida goes on to show that Plato and Socrates, the wise men, are akin to mere sophists and wizards, themselves.

AFTER ALL, PLATO ACCUSES MAGICIANS, WIZARDS AND POETS OF BEING MEN OF WRITING—BUT ISN'T HE ALSO?

**D**errida documents how *both* the wisdom and method of Socrates and the meaningless repetitions of the sophists are called a *pharmakon*. For like the false wisdom, the sophistries, of the sophists, the words of Socrates cause a kind of philosophic mania,

LIKE A NARCOTIC WHICH NUMBS AND PARALYZES WITH THE FORCE OF A STING RAY.

Again, like the virgin whose interior is penetrated by the games of *Pharmacia*, like the *logos*, which is always already penetrated by *mythos*, like speech which is always already a form of writing, "true" Socratic wisdom is always already penetrated in its interior by the false, flim-fmal wisdom of the sophists.

**Q:** And memory?

**A:** Yes, Derrida notes that Socrates calls the evil sort of memory, mere learning "by heart," a *pharmakon*. He says that Plato dreams of a memory that is limitless. But Derrida demonstrates that in order to remember any-*thing, as distinct from other things*, memory would always already have to be contaminated with contrasts and limits—with difference.

AND THE PURE INTERIOR OF THE CITY?

**A:** Yes, the scapegoat is led to the *outside* of the city and killed in order to purify the city's **interior**. But Derrida argues that to be led **out** of the city, the scapegoat must have **already** been *within* the city. Moreover, the ***pharmakos*** or scapegoat is beneficial, like a **medicine** in that he "*cures*" the impurity of the city—but he is at the same time a *poison*, an evil. He is both sacred and accursed.

 ## And that's not all.

The word ***pharmakos*** never *appears* in the Phaedrus, but since Derrida has deconstructed the binary opposition

# inside/outside—

it doesn't matter!

**Q:** So the ***pharmakos***, the scapegoat, is like the ***pharmakon***, the poison, medicine, spell—its meaning is never fixed—and so the meaning of the whole dialogue cannot be fixed.

**A:** Yes. And ***pharmakos*** and ***pharmakon*** are like Thoth, the god of writing. As the god of writing and the secretary of Ra, Thoth doubles for and supplements Ra just as the moon doubles for and supplements the sun, just as moonlight doubles for and supplements daylight and writing doubles for and supplements speech.

rrida says of him:

:annot be assigned a fixed spot in the play of differences. Sly, slippery, masked, ntriguer and a card, like Hermes, he is neither king nor jack, but rather a sort of , a floating signifier, a wild card, one who puts play into play.

god of resurrection is less interested in life or death than in death as a repeti- of life and life as a rehearsal of death, in the awakening of life and in the recom- icement of death. This is what *numbers*, of which he is the inventor and patron, in. Thoth repeats everything in the addition of the supplement: in adding to doubling as the sun, he is other than the sun and the same as it; other than the d and the same, etc. Always taking a place not his own, a place one could call of the dead or the dummy, he has neither a proper place nor a proper name. propriety or property is impropriety or inappropriateness, the floating indeter- mination that allows for substitution and play. *Play*, of which he is also the inventor, as Plato himself reminds us. (D 93)

Q: So this, then, is not just the deconstructive reversal.

A: No, for to simply replace *speech* with *writing* or to replace *poison* with *cure* is to remain locked in the either/or logic of bina- ry opposites. And if writ- ing as *pharmakon* is **both** *poison and cure* **and** *neither poison nor cure* then the dialogue's whole structure of binary oppositions is unstable and unravels in **infinite play, like a wild card, a joker!**

> THE ESSENCE OF THOTH AND OF **PHARMAKON**, THEN, IS THAT THEY HAVE NO ESSENCE. THEY ARE THE PURE POSSIBILITY OF PLAY.

 But if that is so, then all the translations of the *Phaedrus* from the original Greek into other languages must be *inadequate*.

 Yes, because every time translators come to the term *pharmakon*, the meaning of which is *undecidable*, they *decide* and translate it into *one* of its *many* senses, according to the context. Thus they limit it. Derrida's point is that translators should look at *how* **pharmakon** (or any writing) signifies, rather than trying to determine and fix *what* it signifies—because it signifies like a floating card, a wild card, a joker.

## THE DOUBLE SESSION

The second "essay" in *Dissemination* is "The Double Session." The very first page greets the reader with two columns of text. On the left and top, forming a kind of inverted L, is a passage from Plato's *Philebus*. This frames a shorter text nestled within its crook, French Symbolist poet Steven Mallarmé's *Mimique*.

Each passage expounds a different concept of *mimesis* or **imitation**, re[p]resentation.

In Plato's dialogue, Socrates speaks [of] two kinds of *mimesis*, good and ba[d]. Plato believed that true wisdom or knowledge requires a spiritual unve[il]ing of the Ideal Forms that exist beyond external reality. The good painter is the one who paints a faith-ful representation of these images already written in our souls. The b[ad] tape of imitation is like the painter who, without reproducing the Ideal Forms, paints what is false. Thus good artistic representation merely reduplicates or imitates images eternally engraved in the soul.

Mallarmé's text, *Mimique*, based on the elusive figure of the mime, suggests a radically different kind of *mimesis*. For Plato's painter painted a reproduction of a *thing*, a spiritual Ideal Form. But according to Derrida, the mime imitates _nothing_. His *gestures*, and his *facial expressions* ("written" upon his white make up) are a kind of *writing* that imitates *nothing*. As a mime, he *himself* writes *himself* on the unwritten, white page that he is. . . not conforming to any prescription. . .representing *nothing*, imitating *nothing*— but imitation. Neither a representative nor an imitator—he merely mimes mimicry.

The MIME WILL HAVE TO PLAY **BOTH** PIERROT **AN**
COLUMBINE!

"(And he tickles wild, he tic
fierce, he tickles again, he tic
without mercy, then throws
himself on the bed and beco
Columbine. She [he] writhe
in horrible gaiety. One of th
arms gets loose and frees the
other arm, and these two cra
arms start fulminating again
Pierrot. She [he] bursts out
a true, strident, mortal laugh
sits bolt upright; tries to jun
out of bed; and still her [his
feet are dancing, tickled, tor-
tured, epileptic. It is the dea
throes. She [he] rises up on
or twice—supreme spasm!—
opens her [his] mouth for or
last curse, and throws back, o
of the bed, her [his] droopin
head and arms. Pierrot
becomes Pierrot again. At th
foot of the bed, he is still
scratching, worn out, gaspin
but victorious . . .)" (D 201

*Pierrot*
et *Columbine*
après
**WATTEAU**
1684·1721

...He congratulates hims
but soon succumbs to
the tickle, which return
like a vengeful fury,
tickling HIM to death
also.

That's SEXY! But
it seems to me that
the mime is
copying a
sort of
SCRIPT...

**A:** But, you see, the mime was instructed to **improvise** his mimodrama, his(her) writing, with gestures—writing on the white page of him(her)self, writ(h)ing on the white sheet of the bed [*lit*, in French means both *bed* and *read*]—inventing as (s)he went along. And that is not all. We only know of all this by reading Derrida, who read Mallarmé's *Mimique*. But Mallarme only knew about the mimodrama by reading about it in a booklet written by one Fernand Beisser (who had seen the mimodrama)—but the booklet was a *second* edition that wasn't written until several years after the mimodrama! And in the mimodrama the mime merely improvised.

**Q:** So Mallarmé's (and Beisser's and Derrida's and our) retelling of the drama is a process of *mimesis*—

 an imitation of
an imitation of
an imitation of
an imitation

in which there is no original, ultimate point of reference—no original truth—no first principle, no*thing* imitated!

**A:** Yes! Only imitation of imitation.

BUT DOESN'T THIS SUB-VERT PLATO'S CLASSICAL CONCEPT OF **MIMESIS**, OF GOOD IMITATION?

YES. BECAUSE IT DO[ES] AWAY WITH THE IDEA [OF] AN ORIGINAL ULTIMA[TE] PRINCIPLE TO BE IMITATED.

Q: But then, Mallarmé's *Mimesis* is *literature*, and Plato's *Philebus* is *philosophy*. So what is Derrida doing here—literary criticism or philosophy?

A: Derrida is doing something **between** (*entre*) literature and philosophy. You could say that he is deconstructing the binary opposition **between** literature and philosophy, between fiction and truth. After all, he has shown that Plato's **philosophy** describes the good type of *mimesis* as a kind of painting, writing or art. On the other hand he will also show that literature and literary criticism are infected with Platonic philosophy. So Derrida is concerned with the *between*. With what is between literature and philosophy.

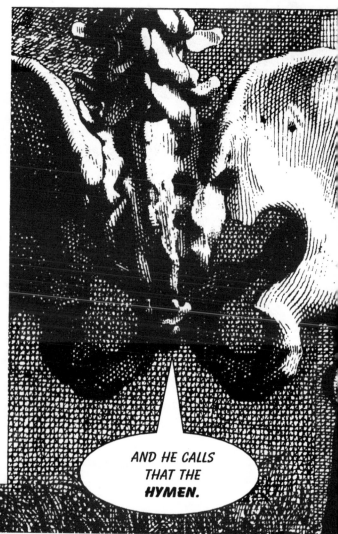

AND HE CALLS THAT THE **HYMEN.**

The **Hymen**! Let's not get personal. So what's the big deal ut a **hymen** anyway?

Well, Derrida is not using "hymen" in the usual sense. He es that it is an *either/or* **between** an *either/or*.

*ELL, ANYONE WHO KNOWS ANY-
THING ABOUT FEMALE ANATOMY
SHOULD KNOW THAT A HYMEN IS
AN EITHER/OR BETWEEN AN
THER/OR WHICH IS BETWEEN AN
'ITHER/OR—AND THAT'S ONLY IF
YOU DON'T TAKE THE WOMAN'S
DESIRE, ITSELF AN EITHER/OR,
'NTO ACCOUNT, NOT TO SPEAK OF
'ER CONSENT OR REFUSAL OR, THE
FOLDS OF HER NEGLIGEE. . .*

it that's how Derrida uses "hymen"—as always *another* **either/or** which is ways between the "last" **either/or**. [So he uses "hymen" to unsettle Hegel's tion of any **synthesis** which lies beyond the **either/or** of the **thesis** and the titesis. He also uses it to unsettle French anthropologist Claude Lévi-rauss's Hegelian notion of a **third element** which mediates between the two embers of a binary opposition.]

So hymen is kind of like *pharmakon*, or *supplement* or the face and candle.

. Yes. Hymen is (n)either virginity (n)or consumma-tion *(n)either* inner (n)or outer. So it is like the ambiguity of the word "pines" in

How mournfully the wind of autumn *pines*
Upon the mountainside as day declines.

You simply can't *decide* which meaning of pines is correct.

93

But then Derrida goes on to say that this **undecidability** is not really due to the various *meanings* of **hymen**: "virginity" (n)or "consummation." And even though his reading of *Mimique* appears to depend upon the meaning of **hymen**—as if everything could be traced back to the **hymen**—Derrida jests that the loss of the **hymen** would not be irreparable. After all, another **hymen** will always pop up.

IN FACT, **HYMEN,** LIKE **PINES** OR **PHARMAKON** OR **SUPPLEMENT** CAN ONLY PRODUCE ITS WISHY-WASHY, UNDECIDED EFFECTS THROUGH SYNTAX.

**Q:** You mean a tax on sin?

**A:** No. Syntax is the *placement* and *grammatical status* of the word in a sentence—not the word's *meaning*.

**Q:** I see! Because *pines* can be either a verb

## How mournfully the wind of autumn pines

or a noun

## Pines upon the mountainside

depending upon where it is in the sentence.

**A:** Yes. And this *shift* in the *syntax, back and forth,* causes a kind of double **folding** process in the sentence, an either/or, a **hymen.**

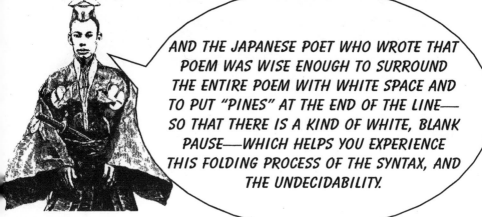

AND THE JAPANESE POET WHO WROTE THAT POEM WAS WISE ENOUGH TO SURROUND THE ENTIRE POEM WITH WHITE SPACE AND TO PUT "PINES" AT THE END OF THE LINE— SO THAT THERE IS A KIND OF WHITE, BLANK PAUSE—WHICH HELPS YOU EXPERIENCE THIS FOLDING PROCESS OF THE SYNTAX, AND THE UNDECIDABILITY.

Gosh! That's beautiful! I want to just go to Japan and, like, you know, just be a Zen nun and just space on the landscape, and like, just write, like haiku and just space into the fold— you know—like while experiencing the whiteness of the cherry blossoms. [pause] Just kidding, of course.

I hope so, because otherwise you will have forgotten your female anatomy! You will have forgotten that Derrida, (and any good Zen master) will have wanted to snap you out of it by saying that spacing is **dancing** between the folds and into the spacing, not just sitting, because there will have been always another either/or, another double fold, another **hymen**, there where you will have been spacing into the folds—as in:

How mournfully the wind
   of autumn pines
upon the mountain *sighed*

95

**Q:** Or how about:

> How mournfully the *wind dove*,
> Autumn, pines
> upon. . .

**A:** Great! Always another either/or or (n)either/(n)or between the last (n)either/(n)or. Always another fold in the hymen. And that's why Mallarmé calls himself "profoundly and scrupulously a syntaxer." The play of meanings in his poetry is always folding like that, and spacing, whitening, through these folds in the syntax.

**Q:** So the **fold**, the **hymen**, and the **blank** and **spacing** are not **things**, or **themes** in Mallarmé's poetry—but **the process of meanings always folding over. Of meanings dissolving in the spacing of these syntactical shifts.** And then arising again. As when the meaning of "pines" (the verb) folds over into "pines" (the noun). So it would seem that neither meaning of "pines" is ever fully present!

**A:** That's right. Each meaning of "pines" is always pining for the other. And Derrida criticizes the Platonic yearning for presence in literary critics such as Jean-Pierre Richard, who, in *Mallarmé's Imaginary Universe* tries to make *fold* into a *theme* in Mallarmé's verse. This **theme** includes a series of words—*folds, wings, pages, sails, plumes, veils*—. Likewise Richard sees in Mallarmé's poetry a theme of whites, of the blank:

THE **BLANK PAPER**, THE **GLACIER**, THE **SNOWY PEAK**, THE **SWAN**. . .

But Derrida's point is that in Mallarmé's poetry the *words* "fold" and "white" are not as important as the *syntactical shifts,* the arising and dissolving of *differences* and meanings, the **folds** in the syntax, the **spacing**, the **hymen** in the reading process, which prevent any of these words, these "folds" or "whites," from ever taking on a simple, single meaning. So that Mallarmé's poetry always remakes itself, folds over itself.

It's like in our diagram. If the white triangles are the series of white or blank "elements" belonging to the "theme" of "whiteness" of "blankness" in Mallarmé's poetry—the unwritten page, the blank paper, the glacier, the snowy peak, the swan—they each seem to be *semic*—to have a *meaning*. But in the diagram, as in Mallarmé's poetry, there is no way of fixing the play of meaning, of any of the white "elements." "They" are always dissolving, folding over, disappearing into a kind of void, a spacing like the void between the two "pines," and then re-*marking* themselves in another configuration—another marking of white or blank triangles. So no particular configuration, no "meaning," is correct. The meaning of each "element", then, remains practically empty, (*asemic*). Perhaps you can begin to understand the following passage by Derrida now. But don't feel bad if you can't. It's typical Derrida:

If there is no such thing as a total or proper meaning, it is because the blank *folds over*. The fold is not an accident that happens to the blank. From the moment the blank (is) white or bleaches (itself) out, as soon as there is something (there) to see (or not to see) having to do with a *mark* (which is the same word as *margin* or *march*), whether the white is marked (snow, swan, virginity, paper, etc.) or unmarked, merely demarcated (the *entre*, the void, the blank, the space, etc.), it re-marks itself, marks itself twice. It folds itself around this strange limit. The fold does not come upon it from the outside; it is the blank's outside as well as its inside, the complication according to which the supplementary mark of the blank (the asemic spacing) applies itself to the set of white things (the full semic entities), plus to itself, the fold of the veil, tissue, or text upon itself. By reason of this application that nothing has preceded, there will never be any Blank with a capital B or any theology of the Text. (D 258)

In the diagram of triangles, in their play, there is no central configuration of "Whites" that could be written with a capital W. The diagram is no longer the expression or representation of any single truth, any central configuration. Nor is it polysemy—having many meanings. It is pre-semantic, before meaning; it is **dissemination**!

# DISSEMINATION 2

So "Dissemination" is *in Dissemination*?

Yes. But "Dissemination" is so challenging
and frustrating that even many
of the best informed readers
have either rejected it or
simply passed it by.

Derrida, in fact, says that the text is "**undecipherable.**" Originally a book review of *Numbers,* a novel by Philippe Sollers, "Dissemination" incorporates within it numerous passages not only from *Numbers*, but to a lesser extent, *Le Parc* and *Drame,* some other novels by the same author. But *Numbers* is no ordinary novel, being composed of numerou fragments:

QUOTATIONS FROM OTHER TEXTS (PASCAL, NICHOLAS OF CUSA, MAO, MARX, BOURBAKI, WITTGENSTEIN)

as well as

*Chinese ideograms,*

(parenthetical asides),

ellipses

DASHES

*diagrams.*

Yet all these are not integrated into a unified theme but grafted onto each other like foreign, mutant branches—so that the story-line inter-reflects itself like a broken mirror.

And "Dissemination" is also a broken mirror, mirroring the broken mirror of *Numbers*, quoting fragments which *Numbers* *itself* a forest of fragments) has quoted, throwing in

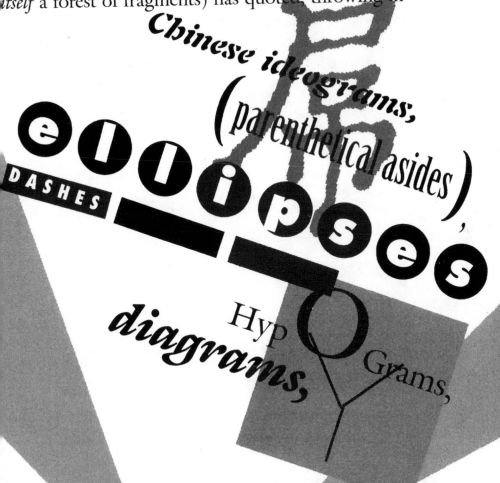

Chinese ideograms, (parenthetical asides), e l l i p s e s DASHES Hyp O Grams, diagrams,

all intertwining with fragments of thought that fly or infiltrate their way in from "Plato's Pharmacy" and "The Double Session." These fragments all mimic *Numbers* like "The Double Session's" Mime who mimes <u>nothing</u>. For *Numbers* is a commentary on what it quotes and on itself, and "Dissemination," supposedly a commentary quoting *Numbers*, is just a jumble of quotations quoting quotations—so there is never an original, primary quote—only "citational effects."

So there appear to be almost two texts here—fragments of a kind of novel made up of fragments, and a fragmented commentary on these fragments. However—Derrida is always interested in a kind of *between*. And one thing that is happening here is that Derrida is trying to deconstruct the binary opposition between *original text* (*Numbers*) and *commentary* ("Dissemination"), because the relationship of an "original" text to its commentary repeats the same kind of binary opposition as in:

**meaning/sound**
**signified/signifier**
**origin/expression**

**Q:** But then, what of the binary oppositions:

**author/book**
**book/reader**
**object/subject?**

**A:** Yes, Derrida sees that these are based on the same metaphysics of presence, and deconstructs or parodies them in "Dissemination."

**A: Q:** So Derrida is not really the author?

**A:** In a certain sense, no. There is no single, unified essay for there to be an author **of.** "Dissemination" is the *interplay* that goes on between *many* texts—not only between *Numbers* and Dissemination—but also works by Plato, Mallarmé, Mao, Marx, Pascal, Nicholas of Cusa, Bourbaki, and Wittgenstein. . . . . So we don't really have two texts or even one text—but really an **infinite** number of texts *that never really **arrive-in** the **present**.*

Ludwig Wittgenstein

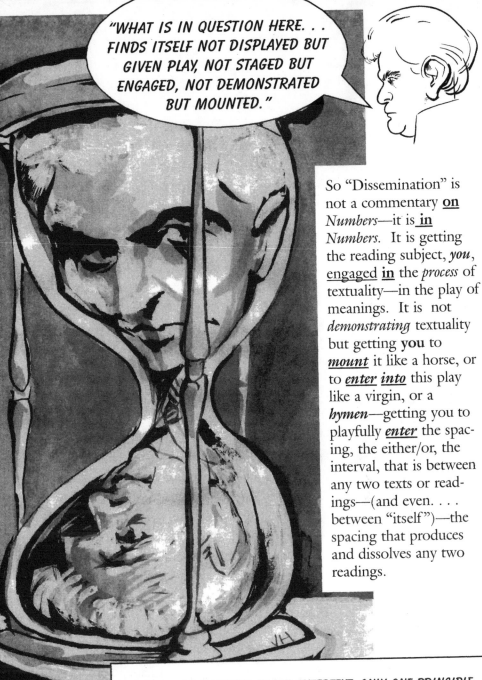

"WHAT IS IN QUESTION HERE. . . FINDS ITSELF NOT DISPLAYED BUT GIVEN PLAY, NOT STAGED BUT ENGAGED, NOT DEMONSTRATED BUT MOUNTED."

So "Dissemination" is not a commentary **on** Numbers—it is _in_ Numbers.  It is getting the reading subject, *you*, engaged **in** the *process* of textuality—in the play of meanings.  It is not *demonstrating* textuality but getting **you** to _mount_ it like a horse, or to _enter_ _into_ this play like a virgin, or a *hymen*—getting you to playfully _enter_ the spacing, the either/or, the interval, that is between any two texts or readings—(and even. . . . between "itself")—the spacing that produces and dissolves any two readings.

"EVERYTHING HAPPENS IN THE INTERTEXT; ONLY ONE PRINCIPLE IS OBSERVED: THAT 'IN THE FINAL ANALYSIS, WHAT HAPPENS IS NOTHING'.  THERE IS ALWAYS ANOTHER BOOK BEGINNING TO BURN AT THE MOMENT 'HE CLOSES THE BOOK—BLOWS OUT THE CANDLE WITH THAT BREATH OF HIS WHICH CONTAINED CHANCE: AND, CROSSING HIS ARMS, HE LIES DOWN ON THE ASHES OF HIS ANCESTORS.'"

**W**hen reading *Numbers*, one of the first things you will notice is that the passages are numbered from 1.0 to 4.100. The number before the decimal point increases from one to four, cyclically. All passages beginning with the number 4 are in the **present tense** (and are in parentheses). So *Numbers* has a kind of squareness to it, it is four-sided, like a page, or a stage with one side open to the *present*. In fact Derrida compares this "**squareness**" of the text to the squareness of a theater, a theater which on the side numbered 4 pretends to *present* the *present*, on the stage of presence, on the stage of the present. But this illusion of presence, of the present, is merely a theatrical effect, the **play** of a ghost, a phantasm.

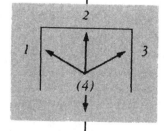

Again, if you contemplate the diagram below, the passage below might become clear. In it Derrida is speaking of the passages in *Numbers* which are in the present tense (the fourth panel), which are numbered 4—but his remarks might also apply to the play of configurations of "seeds" which seem to arise and dissolve on the stage of the present in the diagram below.

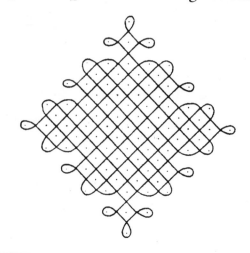

> "THE MOMENT OF PRESENT MEANING, OF "CONTENT," IS ONLY A SURFACE EFFECT, THE DISTORTED REFLECTION OF THE WRITING ON THE FOURTH PANEL, INTO WHICH YOU KEEP FALLING, FASCINATED BY APPEARANCE, MEANING, CONSCIOUSNESS, PRESENCE IN GENERAL. . . . THAT "HORIZON"-VALUE, THAT PURE INFINITE OPENING FOR THE PRESENTATION OF THE PRESENT AND THE EXPERIENCE OF MEANING, SUDDENLY BECOMES FRAMED. SUDDENLY IS A PART. AND JUST AS SUDDENLY APART. THROWN BACK INTO PLAY. AND INTO QUESTION."
> (D 350-51)

TIME IS ALSO A QUESTION FOR DERRIDA.

The appearance of any "present" configuration of seeds is made up of *past* configurations and *future* configurations. Thus Derrida (and Sollers) contrast different **tenses**:

To the **present tense** Derrida contrasts the **future perfect tense**, as in:

# It *will have been said.*

Which contains a kind of contortion of time: a kind of implied **future** and a kind of implied **past** simultaneously, but no **present**— and is much truer to the play of differences.

So "Dissemination" is about the play of meanings that seem to rise up in a kind of illusory present and then fold under like a wave in an ocean.

> EACH TIME, WRITING APPEARS AS DISAPPEARANCE, RECOIL, ERASURE, RETREAT, CURLING-UP, CONSUMPTION.
> (D 339)

So that to give a *commentary* on the text, such as we are attempting here, is to *reinforce* the *illusion* that a <u>present</u> meaning exists—that a text can be *presented*.

When I try to *present* a commentary (as I am doing here), I necessarily resist the *suction* of the play of meanings which attempts to suck any such attempt—which it produces—back into a void. If I try to explain the text, I forget that the *production* of my explanation is already related to its *dissolution*, its *disappearance* into a textual void, a void between any two readings, a void which is always already producing a another reading, and its dissolution.

> THUS IT IS ALWAYS POSSIBLE FOR A TEXT TO BECOME NEW, SINCE THE BLANKS OPEN UP ITS STRUCTURE TO AN INDEFINITELY DISSEMINATED TRANSFORMATION. THE WHITENESS OF THE VIRGIN PAPER, THE BLANKNESS OF THE TRANSPARENT COLUMN, REVEALS MORE THAN THE NEUTRALITY OF SOME MEDIUM; IT UNCOVERS THE SPACE OF PLAY OR THE PLAY OF SPACE IN WHICH TRANSFORMA-TIONS ARE SET OFF AND SEQUENCES STRUNG OUT.
> (D 345)

n engaging us *in* the *play* of textuality Derrida uses several images: ssemination, **the column, the theater, castration** and **mimesis**. But cannot talk about these "images" —saying that they *are* this or that

IT WOULD BE LIKE THE ACTORS IN A PLAY FROZEN LIKE STATUES IN A SERIES OF POSTURES OR GESTURES OR STANCES.

So we must choose between the *play* of textuality, between the play of play, and these frozen statues, these immobile stances—what we would call themes.

cannot say **dissemination** *is* this, or the **column** *is* that. All such gestures main within the surface effect of the *present*, of *explanation*, of *explaining*.

And yet we **can** say what "column" means, we can present the illusion of e present: What is the meaning of *"column?"* It is a kind of phallic nage—a dong—

— )— 屌 — *(DONG: PENIS).*

a column of text, the image of the present; it stands forth like the *present*, like a phallus, *asserts itself* like *explanation*, like the seeming *presence* of meaning, seems to *stand forth*. But this *phallic* effect of pure presence will have been always already *castrated*, cut off. At one moment the surface effect of meaning seems to *stand forth* with meaning, but the next it will have been always already decapitated.

THE COLUMN IS NOTHING, HAS NO MEANING IN ITSELF. A HOLLOW PHALLUS, CUT OFF FROM ITSELF, DECAPITATED. (D 342)

107

It seems as though you are saying that the *text* does all this.

 That's because Derrida deconstructs the opposition:

### text                               reader

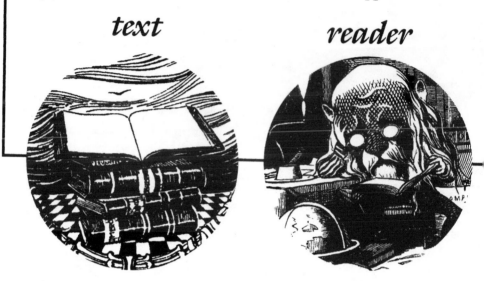

so that as well as you reading *Numbers*, *Numbers* reads, sees and speaks **you**: text and reader, subject and object, become intertwined.

SO, THEN, WHAT IS **DISSEMINATION**?

IF WE SAY THAT "DISSEMINATI
IS THIS, OR IS THAT, WE ARE T
ING TO BOOK IT INTO MEANIN
INTO THE PRESENT. THE WOR
"DISSEMINATION," AS IT IS U
IN "DISSEMINATION" IMPLIES
LINK BETWEEN THE WASTEFUL L
PERSAL OF SEMANTIC (MEANIN
AND SEMEN (WITHIN THE FOLDS
THE HYMEN).

Let us return to our poem:

let's say that at first reading you read *pines* as a *verb*:

ow mournfully the wind of
autumn *pines*
upon the mountainside as
day declines.

It *appears* to have a certain meaning. The wind of autumn *pines* or *longs*.

But then, let's say you suddenly read it as a *noun*:

*ines* upon the mountainside.

W ell *something* must disembed or uproot *pines* from one *appearance of* meaning to the next. *Something* must break whatever it is that fastens *pines* to "longing" and reattach it to "pine(trees)." What is that "Something?" It is the fact that "Pines" will have always been before meaning, will have *never* been rooted *either* in "longing" or in "pine(trees)." For that would be mere

# Ambiguity

the interplay of two meanings. But for Derrida the **meanings (n)either exist (n)or** do not exist. And if this is so, then "*pines*" never *has* nor ever *will* **belong** to any meaning. So if **dissemination** *will have ever* been a thing, it *will have been* that restless tension that *will have disallowed* "*pines*" from *ever having* settled into **any** meaning, from *ever having settled* into the "present" tense, into *being*, into *meaning*.

109

Yet it *will have allowed "pines"* to produce certain effects; it *will have allowed "pines"* to temporarily tease and entertain our yearning, our longing, for certain appearances of meanings—it will have allowed "pines" to perform like a mime on the stage of the "present," presenting theatrical effects: such as *appearing* to present itself as meaning "pine(trees)" or "longing"—but these effects, which stand out, ***phallus-like,*** <u>will have been</u> *always already* castrated. So dissemination <u>***will have meant***</u> no*thing*—for it <u>***will have*** always already produced and **disallowed**</u> its own meanings. In fact, if **dissemination** cannot be defined, it will have been because it will have always already *<u>exploded the</u>* <u>*semantic horizon!*</u>

**Q:** So what we are talking about is a kind of space where dissemination will have been always already taking place.

**A:** Exactly. And that space, includes not only the text but also the reader. It is a scene in the play of presence/absence. In fact one of Derrida's most influential essays is entitled "Freud and the Scene of Writing." It appears in the book *Writing and Difference.*

110

**Freud**

*and the Scene of Writing*

In this essay Derrida traces the progressive refinement in Freud's attempts to visualize how the psyche operates.

*F*reud was trying to visualize a metaphor or model that could explain how memory works—how a pure, virginal surface or substance can harbor permanent traces. For on the one hand, we seem to see things afresh, yet we know that our "fresh," "virginal" perceptions are already colored with traces of our past experience—and that these influence our "present" perceptions.

For instance: If we first see these two faces:

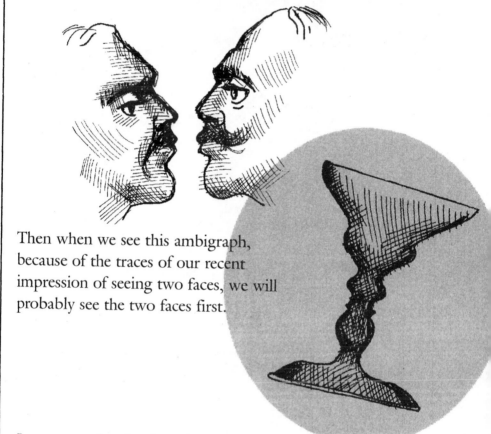

Then when we see this ambigraph, because of the traces of our recent impression of seeing two faces, we will probably see the two faces first.

Just as atomic scientists visualized the atom as a miniature solar system, Freud was looking for an image for how memory works.

It would have to be a somewhat complex image because, Freud thought, the nerves responsible for memory would have to be simultaneously influenced and unprejudiced.

$\mathcal{A}t$ first, around 1895, when Freud wrote "Project for a Scientific Psychology," he thought there must be two kinds of neurons:

**1** **permeable neurons** ($\phi$), which contain no memory and are therefore virginal, and open to perception, and

**2** **memory neurons** ($\psi$), which harbor traces of past experience.

So Freud's first model of *how* memory works was really a concept of *where* memory is located—in different kinds of nerve fibers. But this neurological model proved inadequate and Freud began to think of the psyche as a kind of **writing**—a **script**—**a space of writing**. So though he abandoned the neurological model he never gave up the concept of **location**.

Then, in *The Interpretation of Dreams* (1900), Freud noted that dream images and symbols are a kind of non-phonetic writing.

$\mathcal{Q}$: Non-phonetic writing?

$\mathcal{A}$: Yes. Phonemes are sounds. Each letter of the Roman alphabet that we use spells out a sound. But there are also non-phonetic, non-sound, scripts such as

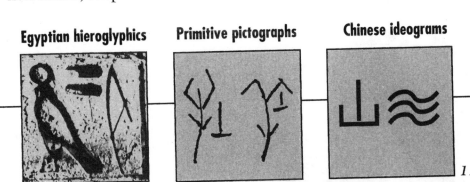

**Egyptian hieroglyphics**   **Primitive pictographs**   **Chinese ideograms**

$\mathcal{F}$reud wrote that the Egyptian priests were the first interpreters of dreams. They believed that since the Gods had given them **both** dream **and** hieroglyphs, that the stuff of **dreams** and the stuff of **writing** were basically **the same mode of expression.** Freud observed that, like Chinese ideograms, dream symbols can contain two or many more meanings.

THE CHINESE IDEOGRAMS

CAN MEAN MOUNTAINS AND STREAMS, OR THEY CAN MEAN THE LANDSCAPE PAINTING.

SIMILARLY IF YOU DREAM AN IMAGE OF A SKINNY COW, IT MIGHT MEAN THAT YOU GREW UP ON A FARM DURING A DROUGHT OR THAT YOUR RELATIONSHIP WITH YOUR MOTHER WAS NOT NOURISHING, OR THAT YOU WERE NOT BREAST FED.

$\mathcal{F}$inally, in "Note on the Mystic Writing Pad" (1925), Freud arrived at the image of memory that Derrida finds meaningful.

THE MYSTIC WRITING PAD WAS A CHILDREN'S TOY IN FREUD'S TIME—MODERN CHILDREN STILL PLAY WITH AN UPDATED VERSIONS OF IT.

The Mystic Writing Pad consisted of three layers. On the bottom was a wax slab. Covering this surface was a sheet of wax-paper—and on top of this was a piece of clear celluloid. A child could "write" or draw on the Pad with a sharp stylus—and "erase" these marks by peeling back the covering sheets, starting from the unattached lower end. The wax slab was like the unconscious because it retained permanent traces of whatever was inscribed on it. The celluloid and translucent sheets were like the conscious mind.

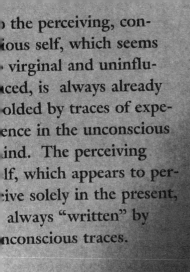

the perceiving, con-
ious self, which seems
virginal and uninflu-
ced, is always already
olded by traces of expe-
ence in the unconscious
ind. The perceiving
lf, which appears to per-
ive solely in the present,
always "written" by
nconscious traces.

But aren't these
traces, themselves,
influenced by former
traces, etc., etc.?

Yes. And you can see why no perception, then, is unpollut-
ed, virginal. Pure perception does not exist. All perception is given meaning by a kind of pre-existing *writ-*
*ing,* by the traces of previous experiences which themselves were influenced by the traces of previous
experiences, etc. And this writing, because unconscious, is a writing that exists before speech.

115

Déconstruction *a la* Derrida often relies upon the play of ambiguous "non-concepts," the meaning of which is at least double. Like the figure of the candle and the faces, these resist being reduced to a single, stable meaning. Derrida employs a whole series of these playful inventions:

| | |
|---|---|
| *pharmakon* | poison/antidote  (in his reading of Plato) |
| hymen | virginity/consummation; inner/outer (in his reading of Mallarmé) |
| supplement | surplus/necessary addition (in his reading of Rousseau) |

But Derrida's most famous non-concept is
# *différance—*
## (difayRAHNS)
which is also the subject of an influential lecture and
essay "Différance," he delivered in 1968.

*Différence* (with an e) is crucial
for Derrida because it was an important
concept for those thinkers who influ-
nced Derrida—Nietzsche, Freud,
Husserl and Heidegger.  It was especial-
y important, however, for Ferdinand de
aussure for whom language as a system
f differences is an important concept in
tructural linguistics.  In his *Course in
General Linguistics* Saussure asserts that
anguage is based on **relation**—that
vords produce meanings because they are
lements in a system of differences.  In this
ystem there are no positive elements—no element that can be called
imply *itself*.

For instance, the mark **A** has no
meaning in-and-of itself, it becomes
"itself" only as an element in a system of differences

It becomes "itself,"——"a" or "h"—
—depending on its relationship to
other marks ( "c" and "t" / "t" and
"e") in the same system.

SO ITS "PRESENT" MEANING DEPENDS UPON ITS RELATIONSHIP TO WHAT IT IS *NOT*.

YES. SO DIFFÉRANCE INCLUDES THE MEANING OF DIFFERING, OF BEING DIFFERENT FROM SOMETHING ELSE. BUT THIS IS NOT DIFFERENCE IN THE USUAL SENSE. FOR INSTANCE, IF I SAY THAT THIS CROISSANT IS DIFFERENT FROM THAT COFFEE CUP, THERE ARE TWO THINGS HERE THAT HAVE DEFINITE QUALITIES. THE COFFEE CUP IS NON-EDIBLE. THE CROISSANT IS EDIBLE, ETC.

What DOES she see in this creep?

It's all that high-falutin' VERBIAGE. Girls just EAT IT UP!! Wait-does that mean she's eating the WORD "croissant"?

But the mark **A** in

$$\begin{matrix} & \mathbf{T} & \\ \mathbf{C} & \mathbf{A} & \mathbf{T} \\ & \mathbf{E} & \end{matrix}$$

is not a thing in-and-of itself. Its identity depends upon its difference from the chain of marks that are strung out in space and time—so that its meaning is never present **in** *itself* but always already deferred, delayed, put off until you have time to cross that space and time separating the **A** from the other marks that give it meaning.

*2:* And that takes time! It's like the definition of a word in a dictionary. "A" says the dictionary, "is the first *letter* of the English alphabet." But to know what "A" is you have to know what "letter" is. And to know what "letter" is ("any *character* of the alphabet") you have to know what "character" means, etc. The meaning of "A" never arrives. It is always put off till later—**deferred** till later.

*A:* Yes. So *différance* includes not only the meaning "to **differ**"—to be different from something else—but to **defer**, to delay, to put off till later.

*118*

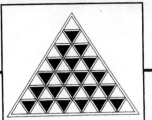

So again, its like our triangles:

Each configuration of triangles that appears is different from other configurations of triangles. But no configuration—as it rises up like a wave—is a positive element, referring only to *itself*—because it is emerging from the *trace* of a "past" configuration and is always already being dissolved into a "future" configuration—leaving only a *trace* of itself. So there is never anything **present**—only *traces* of *traces*.

So *différance* is?

Any attempt to *define* **différance**, which is **not** a word or a concept, involves one in a logical contradiction. For like Derrida's other hinge mechanisms (*pharmakon*, *supplement*, *hymen*, etc.) it is ambiguous. Its play hinges on at least two meanings.

Yet, no meaning of *différance* **ever** arrives, because it is always already **suspended** between two meanings: "to differ" and "to defer"—without ever settling into one or the other.

And if the meaning of *différance* is (n)either "**to defer**" (n)or "**to differ**" —then there is no stable meaning that can ground it in the present—that can stabilize its shape-shifting. It will always dance around like a trickster. It can never be reduced to any one meaning at any one time. If there were some stable presence or meaning that could fix the meaning—the entire "philosophy" which hinges on *différance* would be in error, and would not need pivotal, hinge mechanisms such as *pharmakon*, *hymen*, *supplement* and *différance*.

*Q:* But if *différance* is such a key "non-word" or "non-concept"—and if it is so important in literary studies—then it must—by this time—have degenerated into a kind of buzz word that could be applied to just about any situation.

*A:* Yes. *Différance* was, perhaps, at one time, a disruptive force in Derrida's readings—but has become somewhat tamed—turned into something of a concept. Derrida, though, recognizes the danger of this logocentric tendency and thus is always inventing a new series of roughly equivalent non-concepts (such as *pharmakon, supplement, hymen*). But it is important to note that these terms arise out of the specific books Derrida is reading, wherein they perform very specific tasks, and are not meant to be imported into and applied to other texts, though you wouldn't probably get thrown in jail for using *pharmakon*, for instance, in a literary analysis of Hawthorne's "Rappaccini's Daughter."

*Q:* But why does Derrida spell *différance* with an "a" *-ance*?

*A:* *Différence* in French is spelled the same as in English—with an *-ence*. Derrida intentionally misspells it as *différance* (with an *-ance*) as if it made no *différence*—because after all—he is delivering a **speech**—and speech is supposed to be more effective than writing in communicating the speaker's meaning. But is it? After all, when **spoken**, you cannot tell the *différence* between the "e" and the "a"—*différence* and *différance* **sound** the same in French.

ONE CAN TELL THE DIFFÉRANCE BETWEEN DIFFÉRENCE AND DIFFÉRANCE ONLY IN WRITING!

When **spoken** the *différance* is lost. Thus (the) *différance* can be seen, but not heard. You could say that this is writing's revenge upon speech for having been marginalized.

**Q:** So whether Derrida says *différence* or *différance* in his speech, the audience does not know the *différance*. A simple "meaning" of *différance* can never arrive—it is always already suspended—playing between **differing** and **deferring**—and this suspension creates a kind of <u>interval</u> or <u>blank</u> in space and time that underlies all cases of differing—of distinction—all writing.

**A:** Yes. So the play *différance* produces and undermines all pairs of binary opposites such as

nature/culture

man/woman

poison/cure

**Q:** But if *différance* underlies and produces differences, isn't it like a God or like Being?

**A:** Derrida has warned that it is wrong to think of *différance* as some kind of God of negative theology.

**Q:** Negative theology?

***A:*** Negative theology is theology, talk about God, that takes the form: God is *neither* x *nor* y but z. So when Derrida says that *dif-férance* is *neither* a word *nor* a concept—and that there is no name for what différance "is"—it is not because *différance* is some supertranscendent, mystical essence in the Great Beyond. When Derrida says that *dif-férance* is older than Being or God or any name of God, he is not making a religious statement, a theological statement, but a linguistic one. In order to say "God" you must use the word "God" in a system of differences. *Différance* is not some mystic, unnamable Being. *Différance* does not **exist**.

> BUT DOES THIS MEAN THAT GOD DOES NOT EXIST?

***A:*** By its very nature *différance* and deconstruction can make no statement about the *reality* or *non-reality* of God. But if someone were to use the word Krishna, or Christ or Kahuna or X in an attempt to center or ground their myth or philosophy or theology or war in some stable, unchallengeable meaning from the transcendental Great Beyond, then that central name or concept would be vulnerable to deconstruction. Deconstruction will always subvert the central, authoritarian position that the name Krishna or Christ or X assumes—but it can make no claim about the reality or non-reality of any God. Deconstruction can never prove that there "is" or "is not" a God, but can only unsettle any absolute claim or denial. It is neutral and evenhanded in unsettling all claims of existence or non-existence.

> VIVA LA DIFFERANCE!

> EXISTENCE OR NON-EXISTENCE! THAT'S PRETTY HEADY STUFF. LET'S DRAW THE CORK OUT OF AN OLD CONUNDRUM, AND WATCH THE MEANINGS FIZZ!

$G$*las* is an unusual book. (The word *"glas"* means deathknell of a bell, as in Thomas Gray's poem, "Elegy Written in a Country Church Yard": "The curfew tolls the knell of parting day...") *Glas,* the book, has managed to rouse the ire of many professional academic philosophers. Among other things, it stages a kind of linguistic air battle between philosophy and literature. Two columns of text are printed side by side. On the left-hand side we find Philosophy—embodied by the German philosopher Hegel, who believed that the bourgeoisie family was an embodiment of Absolute Knowledge. In this perfect family, the domain of reason belongs exclusively to the father, and the marginalized woman is left with the roles of wife and mother. Derrida suggests that these gender roles underlie philosophy's notions of how knowledge should be passed down through strictly controlled channels. These roles also provide a foundation for the authority of the name, the signature and the author.

ON THE OTHER HAND. IN THE RIGHT-HAND COLUMN OF GLAS WE FIND LITERATURE, AS EMBODIED BY THE WRITINGS OF JEAN GENET, THE FRENCH HOMOSEXUAL AND THIEF WHOSE WRITINGS CELEBRATED THE VERY OPPOSITE OF FAMILY VALUES.

Just remember, *Die* FRUIT ist der Dialektikal NEGATION! VON DER FLOWER.

By juxtaposing the two columns of text Derrida **forces** the reader to engage in the "air battle" between pure philosophical "truth" and perverse literary "freeplay."

Derrida plays upon the names of Hegel and Genet. Their names mutate, generating all kinds of effects that play somewhere between literature and philosophy. Hegel, as some readers will know, said that knowledge proceeds ever upwards through dialectic. That is, a diagogue between a thesis, and an antithesis, which results in a systhesis. But in Derrida's hands, the name Hegel mutates into the soaring *aigle* (Eagle) ascending on the wings of dialectic, turning and turning ever upwards in spirals of **thesis**, **antithesis** and **synthesis**, conflict and resolution, until it nests in Ultimate Harmony, in the mountain peak of Absolute Reason.

But then there is the other column. Genet's column. Literature's column. Disrupting the upward flight of this Hegelian Eagle of Philosophical Truth, turning and turning in its widening spirals, there blossom, like vast aerial gardens of anti-aircraft explosions, the "Flowers" (Genet in French sounds like *genêt*, a kind of flower) of Genet's prose, of Literature. The flower power in this instance being Genet's blossoms of metaphors and puns seductively unfolding their colorful eddies, ruffles and dark labyrinths.

y putting both on the same page, Derrida forces the reader to experience the literary effects, the unintentional connotations and insinuations and metaphors that blossom up in explosions of meaning from within even the most rigorously unruffled philosophical prose. These explosions, of course, disrupt the upward spirals of the Eagle of Hegelian philosophy.

**Q8** Does this mean that Derrida is *against* concepts, *against* philosophy, and *for* metaphor, *for* literature?

**A8** No. In fact, *Glas* and "The Double Session" have been read in that way—but remember, Derrida is always interested in the **between**. He is interested in something between Philosophy and Literature which is (n)either Philosophy (n)or Literature. He forces us to see how each contains the other, for philosophy may contain literary metaphors, but *metaphor* is itself a philosophical concept!

125

# Signéponge/Signsponge

In *Signéponge/ Signsponge* Derrida deconstructs what he calls "the law of the proper." He does so by playing upon the possible meanings of the French word *propre*, which include "literal meaning," "proper," "cleanliness," and "property"—all of which Derrida associates with proximity and presence.

WHAT, THEN, IS A PROPER NAME?

**A:** According to Derrida, a proper name ought to have no meaning. It should, properly, refer to nothing but what it names. The name Walt Whitman ought to refer only to the great American bearded bard with his hat cocked to one side, loafing and inviting his soul, observing a spear of summer grass. His name should sing, properly, nothing but a "Song of Himself," celebrate nothing but Walt Whitman. The name "Walt Whitman" should say

I EXIST AS I AM, THAT IS ENOUGH.

But since names are **words** caught up in a **system of language**, they always begin to take on meanings, to start making sense, to contradict themselves. They are not supposed to make sense. Yet, non-sense, non-meaning, is always already contaminated with sense, with meaning. Thus "Whitman" has always already been singing of something other than itself. The song of Whitman's self has always already been self-deconstructing. For "Whitman" contains the words "whit" and "man." As in

I DON'T GIVE A WHIT, MAN.

In *Signéponge/Signsponge* we see that the **proper name** is always, already divided, **im-proper**, in the same way that *Words*worth contains "words" with meanings, and that there is a "joy" in Joyce, and that some readers read "Jacques Derrida" as riddled with a "Jack DaReader" (like Jack the Ripper). In Derrida's reading, the signature of the French poet Francis Ponge mutates, improperly. For if a name is a symbol of authority, a signature is even more uptight. We sign our name on checks and legal contracts. We don't want our signature to change into something or someone different. That would be improper and unclean and might involve loss of property.

Yet, in French you cannot hear the difference between

<u>signéPonge</u>
which is to say, Francis Ponge's signature, and
<u>signe éponge</u>
a sign sponge, a sponge that wipes up signs, words.

So, in the same way that Whitman can change into "I don't give a whit, man," Ponge's proper signature—his *signé* Ponge, always already has changed into an improper *signe éponge*—a sign sponge. It is always already a dirty *signe éponge* (sign sponge) even when pretending to act, properly, as a signature, a *signé* (signed) Ponge, it realizes its incapability of cleaning up even its own act.

For the function of a sponge *is* to clean—but this *signe éponge* is only a dirty difference (from the proper, clean *signé* Ponge), so how can it clean? This dirty *éponge* can only pretend to clean up, to expunge, the dirt of improper differences—because it is always only a dirty *éponge*, an improper ponge.

This very improper *signe éponge*, then (which sounds like, the proper, *signé* Ponge) plays like the very improper *différance* (which sounds like, the proper, *différence*), creating and dissolving an array of effects that dance between proper and improper, philosophy and literature, sameness and difference.

# The Truth in Painting

**I**n 1987 we find Derrida painting with a broader palette. We now find him turning his attention to aesthetics, philosophical talk about art.

In "Parergon," the first essay in Truth in Painting, Derrida explores the frame, the *parergon*, which marks the border between the work of art and whatever lies outside it.

That branch of philosophy called aesthetics has always been one such frame, attempting to master art—to enclose it in the circle of its own talk—to frame it. Derrida assigns himself the task of deconstructing that circle or frame.

**Q:** But how can Derrida's deconstruction that circle or frame escape from simply redrawing, or reconstructing another philosophical circle or frame around art?

Under Derrida's scrutiny *parergon*, frame, becomes another expression of the type: *différance, supplement, hymen, pharmakon. It is neither simply inside or outside, inside and outside nor inside nor outside. In the final analysis the parergon does not even exist!*

**A:** Deconstruction seeks neither to reframe art with some perfect, apt and truthful new frame, nor simply to maintain the illusion of some pure and simple absence of a frame. Rather it shows that the *frame* is, in a sense, also *inside* the painting. For the frame is what "produces" the object of art, is what sets it off *as* an object of art—an aesthetic object. Thus the frame is *essential* to the work of art; *in the* work of art. For without it, the work of art is not a work of art. Paint a $5,000 abstract painting on a railroad boxcar and nobody will pay a cent for it. Take a torch, remove the panel of the boxcar, install it in a gallery, and it will be worth $5,000. It will be art because it is now framed by the gallery. But at the same moment that the frame *encloses* the work in its own protected enclosure, making it a work of art, it becomes merely ornamental—*external* to the work of art. Thus is the frame central or marginal? Is the frame inside the work or art, essential to it, or outside the work of art, extrinsic to it?

# Restitutions of the Truth in Pointing

I'D KNOW THOSE SHOES ANYWHERE!

In another essay, "Restitutions of the truth in pointing [*pointure*]" Derrida explores the social, political and philosophical values intruding upon the supposedly pure realm of art and art talk.

The art Derrida has in mind is Van Gogh's painting *Old Shoes with Laces*. What we witness in this essay is Derrida's reading of American art critic Meyer Schapiro critiquing Martin Heidegger's analysis of the painting. Heidegger sees the shoes as obviously belonging to a peasant woman. Shapiro, on the other hand, is equally convinced that the shoes in the painting belong to a city dweller—most probably Van Gogh—himself.

**:** Does Derrida take sides?

**:** No. Derrida, characteristically, is not interested in taking one side
the argument or the other. Instead, he wants us to notice that, on the
surface, both views of the shoes, Heidegger's and Schapiro's, only *seem*
be neutral. Derrida's point is that philosophical talk about art, aesthetic discourse, always involves values, interests and issues from outside
is supposedly pure and neutral aesthetic realm.

errida goes on to point out that neither analysis is as neutral as it
eems. Schapiro, for instance, accuses Heidegger of simply projecting his
wn philosophical fantasies onto the painting. Schapiro, on the other
and, posing as the neutral scholar-critic, who only wants to take the
hoes from Heidegger and the peasant woman and restore them to Van
Gogh, is not so neutral either. For Schapiro had originally learned of the
Heidegger essay from a fellow professor at Columbia, Kurt Goldstein.
But Goldstein had spent time imprisoned in a Nazi prison camp in 1933
before fleeing to America. It is obvious that for Goldstein and Schapiro,
Heidegger's essay has disturbing Nazi overtones.

Derrida argues that "outside" issues such as this,
purely external to art and aesthetics, always enter
in when philosophers, critics and art historians
attempt to point out the **truth** in painting.

One task of deconstruction, then, is to dig out the **hidden** motives in art talk that attempts to point out the **truth** in painting. For social, political and economic issues always intrude *in* the painting.

**Q:** Well it seems that there is an undecidability about the shoes. Do they belong to the peasant woman or to a city dweller? And isn't this undecidability a kind of hymen? In fact the shoes seem to form a kind of female sexual organ between them.

**A:** Derrida wants to tease out this doubleness, this undecidability. He points out that both Schapiro and Heidegger assume there is a wearer, and that the shoes are therefore a *pair*. But, as Derrida comments, the title *Old Shoes with Laces*, does not mention any *pair*. And if they are not a pair, then do they even belong to one person, to an undivided person? And if not, then how could one restore them to their proper owner? And what would be his/her gender? The shoes themselves are phallically pointed, but in their hollowness, suggest a vagina.

# +R (Into the Bargin)

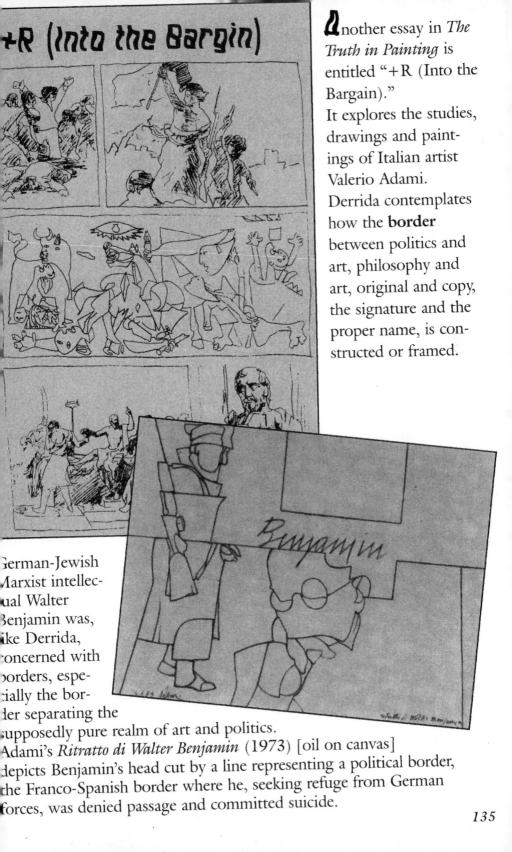

Another essay in *The Truth in Painting* is entitled "+R (Into the Bargain)."
It explores the studies, drawings and paintings of Italian artist Valerio Adami.
Derrida contemplates how the **border** between politics and art, philosophy and art, original and copy, the signature and the proper name, is constructed or framed.

German-Jewish Marxist intellectual Walter Benjamin was, like Derrida, concerned with borders, especially the border separating the supposedly pure realm of art and politics.
Adami's *Ritratto di Walter Benjamin* (1973) [oil on canvas] depicts Benjamin's head cut by a line representing a political border, the Franco-Spanish border where he, seeking refuge from German forces, was denied passage and committed suicide.

135

In writing about Adami's *Studies for a Drawing after Glas*, Derrida discusses the tendency of art talk to want to master or enclose the work of art, and how the work of art resists being imprisoned in words. He renames Adami's drawing *I* (*Ich*).

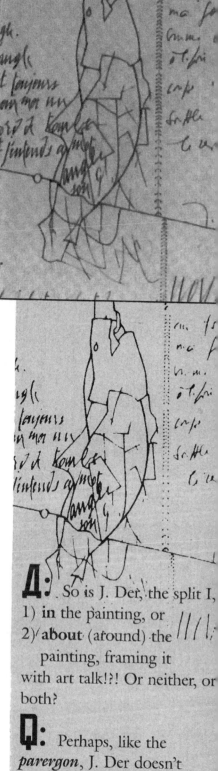

**Q:** But isn't that "J. Der" part of Derrida's signature, in the painting?

**A:.** Yes. But it is only part of "J. Derrida," (only part of the "I"). Actually, Derrida is trying to suggest how a unified self or simple "I" is impossible. He does this by showing how *proper* names are *improper*. Here, in Adami's drawing, which Derrida has renamed "I," is only a half-name—J. Der— which is never fully itself.

**Q:** But the essay and drawing are never fully, originally themselves, either. They are split from the "beginning"

**A:** How's that?

**Q:** Because the essay by Derrida is *about* the drawing which *contains* "J. Der," which is *about* J. Derrida, who is writing about the painting—which he has renamed "I", which contains "J. Der"——-ad infinitum.

**A:** So is J. Der, the split I, 1) **in** the painting, or 2) **about** (around) the painting, framing it with art talk!?! Or neither, or both?

**Q:** Perhaps, like the *parergon*, J. Der doesn't exist!

136

# THE POST CARD

In this volume we find Derrida at Oxford, at times immersed in public and private seminars, at others shut up in the Bodeleian Library reading randomly and creating a grand literary-philosophical farce. For *The Post Card* is supposedly written on the backs of a series of "postcards" addressed to various people—some real, some fanciful. Each of the postcards supposedly bears the same drawing on its front, a reproduction of a thirteenth century illustration depicting Plato, standing behind Socrates, who is seated at a writing table, writing.

WELL, OBVIOUSLY SOMEBODY GOT IT WRONG, BECAUSE SOCRATES DIDN'T WRITE. PLATO DID. IF ANYTHING, PLATO WAS THE STENOGRAPHER!

YES, THIS VIOLATES OUR WHOLE CONCEPT OF PHILOSOPHY. BUT THEN POSTCARDS AS POSTCARDS, VIOLATE PHILOSOPHY'S DESIRE TO COMMUNICATE ETERNAL TRUTHS INDE-PENDENT OF TIME AND SPACE—FOR POST-CARDS ARE ABOUT CIRCUMSTANCES, ABOUT TIME, ABOUT PLACE. THE VERY NATURE OF THE POSTCARD VIOLATES PHILOSOPHY'S INTEREST IN TRANSMITTING RECEIVED TRUTHS THROUGH OFFICIAL CHANNELS—FOR POSTCARDS ARE NOT PRIVATE. THEY CAN BE READ BY ANYONE—AND THUS MISREAD. THIS IS DERRIDA'S WAY OF SAYING, THEN, THAT MERE CIRCUMSTANCES ALWAYS INFLU-ENCE THE SUPPOSEDLY UNIVERSAL AND ETER-NAL TRUTH CLAIMS OF PHILOSOPHY.

Despite his efforts to deny such perceptions, for many years Derrida was viewed by many Marxists as non-historical and non-political.

Then, in October of 1991, scholars at the Center for Ideas and Society at the University of California's Riverside campus decided to hold a multinational, multidisciplinary conference:

J acques Derrida, being one of the most famous contemporary philosophers, was invited to present the plenary address, which formed the basis of *Specters of Marx*, his most visibly political statement to date. But if the tone of these remarks on Marx is serious, because it touches on serious issues, it is equally playful and humorous. For *Specters of Marx*, besides addressing problems concerning Marx and Marxism, stages a kind of **seance**, conjuring up a number of specters, ghosts, spirits, hauntings— which it then attempts to deal with through a kind of **hauntology**—a kind of logic of the ghost. **Hauntology**, another Derridean invention, sounds the same in French (*hantologie*) as ontology (*ontologie*), because the "h" is silent.

# ONTOLOGY

is what takes place when a philosopher sits around wondering about Being, wondering about the very Foundation of Existence, from which all arises, wondering about Rock-Bottom Reality.

# HAUNTOLOGY

on the other hand, involves keeping company with Non-Reality: ghosts, levitating tables, specters. Hauntology deals not with Being, not with Ultimate Reality but with kinds of non-being— the kind of beings that haunt the space between being and non-being, between life and death.

If any configuration of triangles that appears is "life," and if, after its inevitable dissolution, another configuration arises which is "death,"—then to keep company with what happens between "life" and "death," between any two configurations, must involve communication with mere fantasies—with ghosts—with spirits—with the spectral—with mere traces of traces, with the appearance and disappearance of apparitions that, like Hamlet, seem caught up in contemplating the meaning of "to be or not to be," which fleetingly appear to be, but then flicker before the vision, dissolve, and are/not.

or Derrida, attending to, keeping company with these specters between two ings (like life and death; being and non-being) is political. It is political ecause attending to these ghosts means attending to the "Other." This is done the name of justice, and entails responsibility. This **hauntology**—this logic f the ghost, goes beyond the logic of binary oppositions—such as:

# LIFE/DEATH
# TO BE/OR NOT TO BE.

Derrida informs us that the first **noun** in Marx's *Communist Manifesto* is "specter." "A specter is haunting Europe, the specter of Communism," begins the *Manifesto*. And all the powers of old Europe have formed an alliance to conjure away—to exorcise that specter—just as, since the fall of the Berlin Wall, there has arisen a lot of talk aimed at getting rid of the ghost of Marxism, forever. There is a desire to conjure it away, to exorcise it. This talk assumes that Marxism is simply dead—and that the liberal democracies such as the United States are the fulfillment of government on earth. But to haunt (*hanter*), in French, also means "to frequent," and all specters return with a certain frequency.

Derrida, points out, however, that despite their mood of self-congratulation, never have the liberal democracies been in more trouble. One need only look at unemployment, the plight of exiles, the exclusion of the homeless, the economic warfare among states, contradictions in the concept of "free market," the foreign debt, the dominance of the arms industry, the spread of nuclear weapons, inter-ethnic wars, the phantom governments of mafia and drug cartels, and the inequities in international law. Perhaps this is why we want to exorcise the specter of Marxism, because we are so nervous about our own weaknesses.

To these weaknesses of the liberal democracies, Derrida contrasts the spirit of "the New International," a new Marxist spirit inherited from and inspired by *some* of the old spirits of Marxism. And he gives two reasons for a loyalty to a spirit of Marxism:

1) to help close the gap between the *ideals* and the *realities* of liberal democracy, and

2) to *question* the ideals of liberal democracy.

Derrida, though not a Marxist, admits that he, himself, was inspired by a certain spirit of Marxism that insists on self-questioning. Derrida insists that we distinguish this spirit from some other spirits of Marxism—those that bind it to doctrine and to a history of totalitarian repression. Surprisingly, he admits that deconstruction, in the shape it has assumed over the past few decades, would not have been possible, or even thinkable "in a pre-Marxist space" (SM 92). In fact, Derrida sees deconstruction as a more radical form of Marxism.

But it is not only the powers of old Europe that want to conjure away the spirit of communism—Marx does also. For in the *Manifesto* Marx calls for the **incarnation** of the **living reality** of this specter of communism. He calls for it to **present** itself, to **incarnate** itself as the **real**, **final** incarnation and **presence** of the specter. *But this will mark the end of the specter—and of the spectral.*

**Q:** But isn't this just the nostalgia for **presence**, a form of the metaphysics of presence that, as we have discussed, is so prevalent in Western thought? Isn't this just like Rousseau and Levi-Strauss yearning for a natural, primitive society—

*OR LIKE ROUSSEAU'S YEARNING FOR HIS FOSTER-MOTHER'S BREASTS?*

**A:** Yes. But there is a another current in Marx's thought. According to Derrida, Marx envisions the history of Europe as a museum of specters—a parade of **specters** embodying the **spirit** of revolution—and Marx wants to **conjure** these specters in the double sense of **calling them into presence** as examples, and then **exorcizing** them, getting rid of them. Marx, in the end, feels he has no need of these mere poetic phantasms, because the **living reality**, the real **living presence**, of the revolution is better than them. Thus he conjures them up only to conjure them away.

**Q:** So the living **presence** of the revolution seems to have an **ontological** value for Marx. The Presence of the Revolution is Rock-Bottom Reality. And Marx does not want it **haunted** or frequented by mere phantasms, the spirits of the revolutions of the past. He wants **ontology** (*ontologie*), not **hauntology** (*hantologie*). But Derrida suggests, of course, that the supposedly pure **presence** of the revolution, Marx's **ontology,** always already is haunted by the spell of a **hauntology**—always already is haunted by impure specters.

And it is not only in discussing revolution that Marx conjures up specters, only to conjure them away. Derrida illustrates that Marx does the same conjuring trick in his classic discussion of *use-value* and *exchange-value*.

For instance, this ordinary wooden table that we are sitting at has, for Marx, first and foremost a kind of natural *use-value*, which is its *real being*—its **ontological**, Rock Bottom Reality. Because it has this *use-value* you can eat on it. Write on it. Use it as a conversation piece. Drink expresso around it. Discuss its *use-value*.

But when the table becomes a *commodity*, something to be sold—it becomes haunted by a kind of ghost, or specter, a thing which is not a thing—a (no)thing. This *commodity* aspect of the table not only *haunts* the table like a *ghost*, but *levitates* the table to market, where it converses in ghostly communion with other commodities, and flaunts its *exchange-value*.

So the *use-value* of the wooden table is the *original*, **ontological** table. The ghostly, phantasmagoric, **hauntological** spell of the table begins with the *commodity-form* and *exchange-value*. And Marx, after having conjured up this vision of the ghostly *commodity-form* and *exchange-value* of the table, which levitate the table into the marketplace, then attempts to exorcise them. Marx wants to get back to the pure, natural *use-value* of the table. Marx wants to exorcise the spell of the **hauntological** from the **ontological**. He suddenly wants to be an **ontologist**, not a **hauntologist**.

145

**B**ut Derrida questions if this *use-value* of the table is really so pure? Is it <u>really</u> there <u>first</u>, fundamentally, **ontologically**? And if one doubts the original **ontological** purity of the *use-value*—then the **hauntological** spell of *commodity-form* and *exchange-value* always already will have haunted the table. The supposedly "pure" *use value* will have been always already *haunted* by the ghostly possibility of *commodity-form* and *exchange-value*. Always already inhabiting the *use-value* of the table, Marx's **ontology** (*ontologie*) of the table, is the spell of a **hauntology** (*hantologie*). **Hauntology** always already will have haunted **ontology**.

That's clever. Because in French, they sound the same, so the spell of *hauntologie* always already will have haunted, kept company with, frequented *ontologie*, will have always already possessed it, specter-like. In a certain spirit, one can not tell the difference between the two. And isn't this similar to how *différance* always already will have been haunting *différence*!

Yes, and how signe éponge has always been haunting signé Ponge. Marx wants to get rid of **hauntology**. But Derrida says that we are never through with conjuring—we are never finished with **hauntology**. He suggests that perhaps Marx shouldn't chase away the ghosts so quickly. Perhaps he should

frequent them more often, keep company with them for a longer spell. For the spell of *hauntologie*, always already, will have been haunting *ontologie*. This spell is the spirit of the <u>Other</u> and we "should learn to live by learning how not to make conversation with the ghost but how to talk with him, with her, how to let them speak or how to give them back speech, even if it is in oneself, in the other, in the other in oneself: they are always *there*, specters, even if they do not exist, even if they are no longer, even if they are not yet" (SM 176).

# DECONSTRUCTION IN AMERICA

*"America is deconstruction."*
—Jacques Derrida

**T**he institution of American deconstruction began at a now-legendary academic conference at the Johns Hopkins University in 1966. The conference, which was supposed to usher in **structuralism** in the United States, was turned on its head when Jacques Derrida asserted that structuralism was philosophically flawed, and therefore, *passé*. Thus the American era of **post**structuralism began.

The next year, 1967, Derrida published three major works: *Writing and Difference*, *Voice and Phenomenon*, and *Of Grammatology*. Soon he began dividing his time between Paris and Yale, lecturing to audiences that at first didn't know quite what to think of him. He was, after all, a thinker to whom philosophy owed a radical new approach, who, still young, took his place among the great philosophers of history, and who—because he wielded a method which was thought to be nearly incommunicable—was expected to have no heirs.

YET—BY THE EARLY 1970'S OTHER DECONSTRUCTORS AT YALE—AMONG THEM, PAUL DE MAN AND J. HILLIS MILLER—TOOK THEIR PLACE BESIDE DERRIDA, FORMING A THREESOME THAT DISCIPLES SAW AS A LUMINOUS CONSTELLATION, AND DETRACTORS DUBBED YALE'S "BOA DECONSTRUCTORS."

It was really Paul de Man, however, who was the shining example of what came to be known as the "Yale School," who passed like a meteor through the heavens of deconstruction—adapting Derrida's thought to the study of literature. Soon the American study of deconstruction eclipsed its French following, spreading from a handful of universities such as Yale, Johns Hopkins, and Cornell, to revolutionize and politicize literature and humanities departments nationwide, and then worldwide.

**D**errida had always been concerned with collapsing the difference between literature and philosophy. Paul de Man seized upon the literary aspect of Derrida's work and, along with other critics, transformed deconstruction into a method which was only too communicable.

Paul de Man's readings, like Derrida's, locate binary oppositions in texts. But de Man shuns the playful, difficult, dazzling and dizzying Derridean style with its puns and hinge mechanisms. De Man prefers a more conventional prose—sober, rigorous and analytic.

Deconstruction in the de Manian mode demonstrates how a text dismantles its own privileged or traditional meanings. For, according to de Man, the reading of any text deadlocks in a kind of **aporia**, a logjam between the rhetorical and literal levels of meaning.

Rhetorical and literal levels?

Yes. Let's look at the rhetorical and literal
levels of meaning in a passage
from William Butler Yeats's poem
"Among School Children."

O chestnut-tree,
great-rooted blossomer,
Are you the leaf, the blos-
som or the bole?
O body swayed to music,
O brightening glance,
How can we know the
dancer from the dance?

According to de Man, the last line can be read in either of two ways:

**1** **Figuratively**: It becomes a rhetorical question. It says—in effect—
that we *can't* tell the dancer from the dance. That the *form* of the
dance and its *performance* are identical, fused into one, unified. This
is the traditional interpretation.

**2** **Literally**: It assumes we *can* tell the dancer from the dance and
asks us what we would look for in order to distinguish the dancer as
different from the dance. It assumes that the **form** of the dance and
the **performance** of the dance are somehow separate.

*150*

**B**ut the question about *form* and *performance* can **also** be asked of the last line of the poem, itself. How can we distinguish the *literal form* of the line, its literal meaning, from its *"performance"*——the *rhetorical, figurative "dance" of meaning* in the *line*—

IN WHICH IT MEANS EXACTLY THE **OPPOSITE** OF ITS LITERAL MEANING.

For de Man these two contradictory readings reach a deadlock, an **aporia**. De Man calls this stalemate *"undecidability"* or *"unreadability."* Thus the line cannot say anything, mean anything or take any position that it does not also subvert. And because these two meanings of the line exclude each other, any such reading of a text always logjams in doubt, undecidability, **aporia**. The reader, then, is left to choose between the two readings of the line, even though the foundation for making any choice has been removed.

**B**ut if this is true, then none of the established interpretations of texts can be upheld. All reading becomes paralyzed (as by a boa constrictor) in the **undecidability** of meaning. This kind of deconstructive reading became widespread in American universities in the 70's and 80's—a hip new method full of weird sounding buzz words and phrases—a method which was borrowed from by a variety of groups (feminists, gays, ethnic minorities) who perceived themselves as marginalized victims of centralized cultural values. They used the methods and lingo of deconstruction not only to read texts, but to oppose and subvert those established institutions, books or individuals they perceived as their oppressors. Soon theory classes were as important as literature in graduate English programs. And not only were traditional readings of texts deconstructed, but, for instance, in classes on modern literature, formerly marginalized gay, ethnic minority or female novelists might now be substituted for central, dead-white-male authors such as Hemingway or Frost.

**Q:** But doesn't de Man's method of deconstruction fall short? To construct something is not simply to show how a marginalized element can be seen as central, how it can **overthrow** a central element—leading to an *aporia*—to **undecidability**—but to go *beyond* the stand-off between binary opposites now viewing them dancing in a freeplay of differences.

**A:** Yes. Though de Man was a subtle and gifted critic, his type of deconstruction became a commody fit for mass consumption, with deconstructive readings of texts tending to end in *aporias*, deadlocks of meaning, undecidability. But if every reading ends in "undecidability" then "undecidability" reveals itself to be quite decidable, quite mechanical. Political opponents of this type of deconstruction feared that "undecidability" could lead to political inaction and thus to the continuation of the status quo.

In this ambigraph, our attention does not remain deadlocked in the neutral gap between the faces and the candle—but plays back and forth endlessly. So for Derrida, because the system is founded in difference, neither candle nor faces can purge the "other" from its own domain—each contains the "other" within itself. This results not in paralysis but in freeplay.

But it was not because of this distortion of Derrida's approach that de Man's career shone brilliantly, and then crashed like a meteor.

153

**Q:** . What happened?

**A:** Well, for one thing, de Man passed away in 1983, becoming something of a dead white male, himsel But this event did not cause him to be forgotten. If any thing, it only added to the aura of reverence which sur rounded him. Graduate students continued churning ou deconstructive readings in the de Manian mode.

**Q:** Then, what happened?

**A:** Well, those given to deconstruction had always thought of themselves and their approach as revolution ary, iconoclastic and anti-totalitarian. In fact, if all texts are "unreadable" because of an inherent undecidability, then as one Yale-school deconstructor put it "meaning is fascist."

The irony is that the reason de Man's career can be described as meteoric is that its luminosity was eclipsed, four years after his death, by something unforseeable, something horrific, something that stood for all that deconstruction seeks to deconstruct.

**Q:** Well, what was it?

**A:** Paul de Man's continuing radiance was eclipsed by the specter of the swastika.

**Q:** The swastika!

**A:** In December of 1987 a headline appeared in the *New York Times*:

---

# YALE SCHOLAR'S ARTICLES FOUND IN NAZI PAPER

The article declared that Paul de Man, the leading guru of American, literary, deconstruction, from 1940 to 1942, had written articles for a pro-Nazi publication during Germany's occupation of Belgium in World War II.

**Q:** That's terrible!

**A:** Well, it's terribly ironic! Of course detractors of Derrida, of deconstruction, and of de Man, those who had derided Derrida and de Man as boa deconstructors, seized upon this news with a vengeance. It was as if history had delivered into their hands an argument against deconstruction more powerful than any theoretical opposition they could mount. The purest and most holy gurus of deconstruction had, for years, kept silent about de Man's questionable past.

**Q:** Detractors?

**A:** Yes. Deconstruction has tended to inspire either adoration or hatred. For instance, many philosophers tend to think that Derrida has oversimplified the Western philosophic tradition. Other critics seem to think that deconstruction, relying on readings of other texts, is like a parasite. Some call it linguistic nihilism, that it believes in nothing. Some say there are more subtle, less mechanical, ways of reading texts than to start looking for binary opposites. Some say the language of deconstruction is too difficult. Some of those in the establishment blame it for Political Correctness on campuses. Some Marxists think that it is too playful, like masturbation, and not political enough. Some feel that America has rock and roll, the sexual revolution, and the sixties, and does not need deconstruction. Many professors and students do not really understand the (non)concepts of deconstruction—and thus are never able to *critique* deconstruction. They merely learn the buzz words and repeat them like religious dogma, fearing the label of "racist" or "politically incorrect" or simply "unintelligent" if they lapse in these devout recitations. They have tended to make something of a broad religion out of deconstruction, which might be called "deconstructionism."

ALL OF THESE SENTIMENTS, MANY OF WHICH DISPLAY A REAL, BUT UNDERSTANDABLE, IGNORANCE OF DECONSTRUCTION, HAVE TENDED TO MAKE DERRIDA INTO A KIND OF SCAPEGOAT AS WELL AS A HERO, A POISON AS WELL AS A CURE.

THE REVELATION ABOUT DE MAN'S WARTIME WRITINGS CERTAINLY DID NOT WIN DECONSTRUCTION MORE FRIENDS.

But then, more fuel was added to the fire.

A group of leading deconstructors, with Jacques Derrida in the lead, published responses to the de Man writings. To their credit, they did not try to conceal or ignore the accusations. Derrida's response to this news about his close friend and colleague was entitled "Like the Sound of the Sea Deep Within a Shell: Paul de Man's War."

In that response Derrida proclaims that we must respect de Man's right to be different from others and from himself. He also asserts that his main feeling is one of compassion for de Man. He writes we should not judge de Man solely by something he did in his youth, forgetting his contribution of forty years as a thinker, writer, theoretician and professor. He states that any attack or defense of Paul de Man, since it cannot really affect a dead man, is really a disguised attack or defense of deconstruction. And he adds that he would like to weigh the evidence carefully, assuming his responsibility to respond for his late friend, while defending neither de Man nor himself. He states that he doesn't know if this is possible.

Derrida also offers a close reading of some passages from the article in question—an article published in the pro-Nazi newspaper *Le Soir*.

On the one hand Derrida admits that de Man unquestionably sounds like he is on the side of the German forces occupying Belgium.

But, on the other hand, Derrida's reading finds de Man's article "constantly split, disjointed, engaged in incessant conflicts" (SSS 180).

In other words, Derrida simply begins doing to de Man's text what he does best—deconstruct—reading the text against the grain of its obvious meaning and intention, teasing forth the conflicts between sense and implication, showing that the text never means only what it says or says only what it means.

In this way Derrida (on the one hand) condemns de Man for what seems like anti-Semitic language and sentiments. But (on the other hand) Derrida thinks he hears in this same passage the voice of a characteristically nonconformist Paul de Man "coiled up and resonating deep within" this anti-Semitic prose (as within a seashell), voicing a subtly disguised *criticism* of "vulgar anti-Semitism" (SSS 215).

*On the one hand* Derrida finds that de Man *did* write in a pro-Nazi newspaper, blaming Jews for their role in the 20th century disorganization of Europe; that he *did* label Jews as cold, detached, and cerebral, as second-rate writers; and that he *did* suggest a "solution to the Jewish problem" involving mass deportation of Jews. Derrida finds these statements unpardonable.

it then Derrida devotes the next several pages to a kind of constructive reversal.

HE NOTES THAT DE MAN PRAISES GIDE, KAFKA (A JEW), LAWRENCE AND HEMINGWAY IN THE SAME ARTICLE.

Derrida finds this list insolent because these writers are hardly Fascist. One of them is even a Jew. Was this de Man's way of subtly subverting Nazi doctrine? Then Derrida gets suspended in a kind of deconstructive *aporia*, a moment of undecidability concerning the phrase "vulgar anti-Semitism." Does de Man mean that there is a **congenial** as well as a **vulgar** sort of anti-Semitism or does he mean that **all** anti-Semitism is vulgar? Can some strands of de Man's text, in fact, be read as a subtly disguised, non-conformist criticism of all anti-Semitism? Is de Man's text, in fact, subtly pro-Jewish?

GIVE ME A BREAK!

That's exactly what Derrida's critics said. They seized upon "Like the Sound of the Sea Deep Within a Shell: Paul de Man's War" as the example *par excellence* of critical irresponsibility. Many saw it as a shameless apology for de Man, and as a piece that, while claiming that deconstruction is anti-totalitarian, demonstrates its inability to criticise totalitarianism, or anything.

**B**ut they were especially surprised by Derrida's statement that criticism of de Man is equivalent to reproducing an "exterminating gesture." That Derrida saw de Man as a victim of those same totalitarian strategies for which he was condemned. Some of Derrida's critics felt that his response to the de Man scandal was shallow, and more damning to deconstruction than if Derrida had remained silent. For now, in their eyes, the validity of deconstruction as an intellectual force was questioned. How anti-totalitarian and iconoclastic can deconstruction be, they argued, if its followers so shamelessly attempt to defend their heroes by overturning the obvious facts via deconstructive strategies.

Furthermore, they asserted that de Man's reading strategy, which regards texts as "unreadable," as leading to an *aporia*, undecidability, could now be seen as self-serving, as it tends to erase the meaning of his early writings.

**D**errida, who had perhaps become somewhat immune to being blamed for providing a philosophical basis for "political correctness" on college campuses, seemed oblivious to the fact that now he was being politically incorrect, and that any intellectual response he could make, no matter how intelligent or finely nuanced, could not stand up to the intense emotions associated with the relationship between Jews and Germans in World War II.

To all these things, and to the criticism that deconstruction had displayed its inability to fight totalitarianism or anything, Derrida responded philosophically—"What is a thing?" Because, for Derrida, totalitarianism, or any**thing** is not simply itself, but contains the trace of its opposite. But he also responded emotionally, finding his critics' responses to be based on fear, and stated that he, himself, felt fear.

Thus he became so frustrated with the responses of the press and his critics in academia that he wrote "Biodegradables: Seven Diary Fragments", ridiculing what he saw as a non-thinking dismissal of de Man, and unjustified attacks on deconstruction and himself, which, after all, have nothing to do with Nazism.

Well. Now we're getting somewhere!

**A:** How's that?

**Q:** Well, if Derrida has taught us one thing, it is the importance of the marginal. And in this whole discussion, this is the first time that emotion has upstaged intellect and taken center stage since Derrida's childhood.

**A:** And that leads to a Buddhist criticism of deconstruction. Mādhyamika (Middle-Way) Buddhism is a form of Buddhism that uses some of the same arguments as deconstruction, often angering and confusing both Hindus and other Buddhists with its deconstructive logic. For instance the Middle-Way statement that "The Buddha did not teach anything to anyone at any place" (EE 207), does not deny the historical reality of the Buddha, but questions the seeming <u>thingness</u> of things, of people and of places. Like Derrida, the Mādhyamakins have been accused of nihilism—of teaching that nothing exists. But, as a couple of Mādhyamika sayings have it, "When a **thing** is not found, how can there be a **nothing**?" (EE 207) Or "I do not negate any**thing**, nor is there any**thing** to negate" (EE 207)

Like deconstruction, Mādhyamika Buddhism avoids using words and concepts as though they are expressions of some Great Beyond. But instead of attempting to deconstruct central, established institutions, or the metaphysical ideas that underlie such institutions, as does American deconstruction, they aim within, not only at intellectual structures, but more importantly, at the emotional basis of *clinging*.

**T**hrough meditation, the Mādhyamika Buddhist will *first* of all try to deconstruct her own painful emotions—such as anger. Attacked by the deconstructive logic of Buddhism, painful emotions taper off to nothing—just like a Zen riddle.

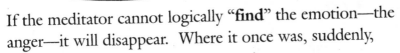

> BY THE WAY—WHAT DO A RAVEN AND A WRITING TABLE HAVE IN COMMON?

If the meditator cannot logically "**find**" the emotion—the anger—it will disappear. Where it once was, suddenly,

there is only emptiness. And once a particular anger, for instance, has been found to be empty, then it becomes easier to realize the emptiness of "other things." Then the meditator may realize: "This is not my beautiful house!" "This is not my beautiful car!" "This is not my beautiful wife!" "All these things are empty!" "And even the *doctrine* of emptiness is empty!" For, like "differance," "emptiness" is not a concept or idea or **thing**—but a tool for deconstructing *clinging*, even clinging to the concept of "emptiness." It follows that there must be no sense of needing to defend the doctrine of emptiness, for intellectual clinging is one of the worst forms of suffering. One should see the emptiness even of emptiness. Thus the meditator finds that there is no underlying basis for any emotion, experience or viewpoint—and with no**thing** to grasp, the mind is free.

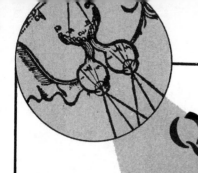

**Q:** So why hasn't psychotherapy adopted deconstructive insights?

**A:** Actually, deconstruction has had an enormous impact in the field of psychotherapy as well. Deconstructive psychotherapy uses an approach to therapy that decenters the traditional relationship between therapist and client. In traditional therapeutic approaches, the therapist considers himself to be the expert. He's the one behind the desk, with the clipboard. He likes to think of himself as a professional with a trained eye. He even thinks that he has access to scientific, objective knowledge—to immaculate perceptions of the client's condition. This knowledge often consists of fixed notions of what makes a healthy or sick psyche. The therapist thinks himself capable of quickly labeling the client as, for example, "fixated anal retentive," "oral incorporative," or "early phallic." But are these really immaculate perceptions or only delusions of certainty?

Deconstructive therapists feel that all knowledge, including scientific knowledge, is influenced by one's perspective—and that any perspective, even a scientific one, is the product of dominant cultural influences and ideologies.

instead of operating from an expert, decisive, certain therapeutic posture, deconstructive therapists come from a curious, collaborative posture—a posture which tolerates ambiguity and confusion, which moves carefully and slowly in defining the problem, which favors the narrative knowledge and vocabulary of the patient, which is careful to discover the client's strengths, and which considers the client to be the expert on how to live her own life. The deconstructive therapist lets the client voice her own story—and uses her own vocabulary in responding to her. Instead of getting the client to behave in a certain way—through teaching, controlling, or confronting the client—the deconstructive therapist opens a space for the client to entertain new ways of seeing herself and her problem.

Whereas traditional therapists assume clients have one essential self which operates in all situations, deconstructive therapists allow the multiple selves and stories of the client to emerge as they are influenced by various contexts. The client may be, for instance, a lover, a parent, a daughter, a colleague, a surfer, and an employer. If clients are not assumed to have one true self, neither are they labeled as "enabler," "blamer" etc.

Should a client attempt to reduce herself to a label such as

"*I AM A DEPRESSED PERSON,*"

then the deconstructive therapist will acknowledge the story but try to open up a space so the the client may see other, marginal, stories that may be more healthy than the central, problematic, story. The deconstructive therapist avoids letting the client reduce herself to one final story, but lets subtle variants of the central story emerge.

One way in which this is done is for instance, to allow the client who labels herself as "a depressed person," to see the depression not as an inborn and essential part of herself, but an external element that can be acted upon.

**Q:** So what happened to deconstruction? Did it die? Or had it just deconstructed itself?

**A:** Neither, and both. Deconstruction, as a process of reading is always producing and dissolving readings. The institution of Deconstruction, per se, may not enjoy the following in American universities that it had in the 80's. Few critics are still churning out the kind of rote deconstructive readings which flooded the journals of past decades. But deconstruction is not dead. Theory, in fact, has become a part of the undergraduate curriculum. In 1992 Barbara Johnson, a prominent voice in feminist deconstruction, delivered a lecture on "the wake of deconstruction." In true deconstructive fashion she played upon the meanings of "wake."

*IT CAN MEAN A FUNERAL, A WAVE ROLLING OFF A PASSING VESSEL, OR AN **AWAKENING**.*

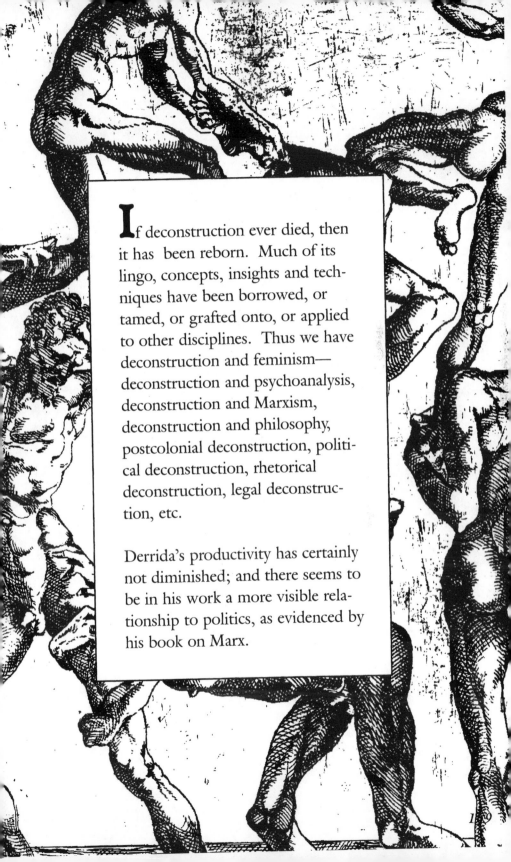

If deconstruction ever died, then it has been reborn. Much of its lingo, concepts, insights and techniques have been borrowed, or tamed, or grafted onto, or applied to other disciplines. Thus we have deconstruction and feminism— deconstruction and psychoanalysis, deconstruction and Marxism, deconstruction and philosophy, postcolonial deconstruction, political deconstruction, rhetorical deconstruction, legal deconstruction, etc.

Derrida's productivity has certainly not diminished; and there seems to be in his work a more visible relationship to politics, as evidenced by his book on Marx.

Barbara Johnson practices a kind of feminist deconstruction, and is best known through two books. In the first, *The Critical Difference*, she applies the de Manian method of "rhetorical" deconstruction to texts by Roland Barthes, Herman Melville, Edgar Allan Poe, and Jacques Lacan. In her second book, *A World of Difference*, she goes beyond the literary framework, applying deconstruction to the world of political differences in gender and race relations. She also examines assumptions and values determining which works are valued and read, and she looks at how criticism functions in institutions. In this way she reads the whole world, not just literature, as a field of difference.

WAS THE LITERARY CANON, ALL THESE BOOKS BY DEAD-WHITE-MALES: SHAKESPEARE, HEMINGWAY, MILTON, PLATO—WAS THE LITERARY CANON WRITEN ON STONE TABLETS BY GOD?

NO, IT WAS CONSTRUCTED BY DEAD WHITE MALES, LIKE ME.

WELL THEN, SINCE THERE IS ONLY SO MUCH TIME IN A SEMESTER—WE ARE GOING TO BUMP HEMINGWAY AND MILTON AND TEACH TONI MORRISON'S _JAZZ_ AND MARY SHELLEY'S _FRANKENSTEIN_. WOMEN AND ETHNIC WRITERS HAVE BEEN MARGINALIZED FOR TOO LONG. AND THEY HAVE JUST AS MUCH RIGHT TO BE CENTRAL AS SHAKESPEARE!

OY VE! WHAT HAVE I DONE!? I WAS JUST BEGINNING TO UNDERSTAND PLATO!

# Architecture

**R**ather than striving for the purity and unity of form exhibited in Modernist architecture, the deconstructivist architect celebrates asymmetry, complexity, contradiction, displacement and incompatibilites of style, function and form. Instead of abandoning ornamentation, she revels in the play of the decorative, the superfluous, the inessential—mixing inside and outside, domestic and public spaces, Modern, Jacobean, Renaissance and French Provincial styles, functional and decorative elements.

The plumbing, for instance, may serve a decorative function on the outside of a structure—a structure which presents the general shape of a Greek Library, but decorated by ornamental Egyptian pyramids and statues of Thoth questioning Corinthian columns—all lighted up with Las Vegas neons. Thus architecture, for deconstructivists, is a way of breaking down the binary opposites of architecture—public and private space, inside and outside, form and function, it is a way of doing philosophy.

But styles are not just randomly mixed, but juxtaposed in such a way that they question each other. A function, such as habitation, living in a space is not simply abandoned, but displaced by ornamentation, by perhaps putting a gargoyle around the cupboard, calling habitation and function into question. In this way architecture ceases being a spatial art or means of providing habitation—becoming an exploration of the play of differences that exceeds space and thus makes spaces and habitations possible and questionable.

172

# LAW

In the legal arena, deconstruction has given birth to a movement called Critical Legal Studies, or CLS, which has caused intra-departmental wars at leading law schools such as Harvard. CLS says that the conventional truth claims supporting laws are based in the biases of the central, powerful class. CLS sets about deconstructing these claims by looking at their central axioms. In the CLS courtroom laws are read like Derrida might read Rousseau. Laws are deconstructed, their ambiguities exposed. Thus any judge may choose either interpretation—even though the basis for making a decision has become problematic.

WHITE MAN'S LAW IS BASED ON THE ASSUMPTION THAT THE WHITE MAN'S GOD IS CENTRAL AND BETTER THAN THE GREAT SPIRIT. BUT WHY NOT THINK THAT THE GREAT SPIRIT IS CENTRAL INSTEAD OF MARGINAL. THEN WHITE MAN'S LAW HAS NO FOUNDATION FOR KEEPING OUR ANCESTRAL LANDS FROM US!

(Author's grandfather)

raditionally, ethnographers have considered themselves to be authorities, professionals schooled in the rigorous methods of gathering the truth about cultures and of transmitting it in a disinterested manner. They have viewed their position as different from that of the missionary, the colonial administrator, the traveler, the trader. After all, they have observed themselves squatting by campfires, where they appeared to themselves to listen objectively, neutrally, scientifically to the natives.

ut in reality many ethnographers only learn a small part of the native
nguage, and see only a part of the native culture—but then they con-
ruct their idea of the whole culture on this basis. Obviously there are
oblems in this. The native may have been just making up fictions in
rder to get some chocolate. The ethnographer may falsely imagine that
is performance is real information. So neither the ethnographer nor
e object of study is so innocent. The ethnographer's descriptions are
ways a graphy—a writing—a translation, a text, and infected with
nexamined cultural forces. His representations of a native culture may
st turn out to be a way of exerting colonial power over them. Thus
me ethnographers have sought to decenter the ethnographic encounter
y becoming aware of these problems and reversing the authority—by
xploring ways to give cultural authority back to the informants them-
lves. One way to do this is to stop relying on a single informant, and
encourage a collaborative ethnography in which native informants col-
ctively stage and produce their own stories, telling these stories through
multitude of different voices, which will not necessarily be in agree-
nent with one other.

# Deconstruction and Fashion

The brainchild of three Belgium arts students—Dries van Noten, Ann Demeulemeester and Martin Margiela, deconstructive fashion was a reaction to the designer and label consciousness of the 80's. The Deconstructive Look involves drab colors, visible seams and linings, and unfinished edges. The fad peaked in the early 90's.

# SELECTED BIBLIOGRAPHY

## Works by Derrida

Abbreviation
Used In Text

"Biodegradables: Seven Diary Fragments." tr. P. Kamuf,
*Critical Inquiry* 15, no.4, summer 1989.

"Différance." tr. Alan Bass, *Margins of Philosophy.*

(D)  *Dissemination.* tr. Barbara Johnson (U Chicago P, 1982).

*Glas.* tr. John P. Leavey, Jr., and Richard Rand, (U
Nebraska P, 1986).

*Of Grammatology.* tr. Gayatri Spivak (Baltimore: Johns
U P, 1976)

*Jacques Derrida* (in collaboration with Geoffrey Blooming)
tr. Geoffery Bennington (U Chicago P, 1992).

(SSS) "Like the Sound of the Sea Deep within a Shell: Paul de Man's
War." Peggy Kamuf, *Critical Inquiry* 14, Spring 1988.

*Margins of Philosophy.* tr. Alan Bass (U Chicago P, 1981).

*Memories: For Paul de Man.* tr. tr. Jonathan Culler, et al. (U
Chicago P, 1989).

*Positions.* tr. Alan Bass (U Chicago P, 1981).

*The Post Card.* tr. Alan Bass (U Chicago P, 1987)

(S)  *Signéponge/Signsponge.* tr. Richard Rand (U Chicago P,
1983).

(SM) *Specters of Marx.* tr. Peggy Kamuf (New York: Routledge,
1994).

*Speech and Phenomenon.* tr. David Allison (Evanston:
NorthWestern U P, 1973).

(WD) *Writing and Difference.* tr. Alan Bass (U Chicago P, 1978)

YOU CAN ALSO FIND ME ON THE WEB!

## Works on Derrida

*Against Deconstruction*. John Ellis (Princeton UP, 1989)
*Derrida*. Christopher Norris (U of Chicago P, 1987).
*Derrida and Deconstruction*. ed. Hugh Silverman (New York: Routledge, 1989).
*Derrida and Indian Philosophy*. Harold Coward. (SUNY P, 1990).
*Derrida on the Mend*. Robert Magliola (Purdue U P, 1984).
*On Deconstruction*. Jonathan Culler (Routledge, 1982).

## Works on Madhyamika Buddhism

"The Clôture of Deconstruction: A Māhāyana Critique of Derrida". David Loy. *International Philosophical Quarterly*, 105 March 1987.
"The Deconstruction of Buddhism." David Loy. *Derrida and Negative Theology*. ed. Harold Coward and Toby Foshay SUNY, 1992).
(EE) *The Emptiness of Emptiness*. C. W. Huntington, Jr. (U of Hawaii P, 1989).
*Emptiness Yoga*. Jeffrey Hopkins (Ithaca: Snow Lion, 1987).

# INDEX

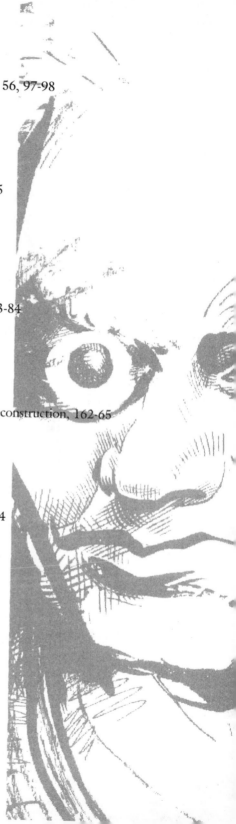

VH